THE TABERNACLE

ii

High Priest.

THE TABERNACLE

ITS PRIESTS AND ITS SERVICES

Updated Edition

WILLIAM BROWN

HENDRICKSON PUBLISHERS

The Tabernacle: Its Priests and Its Services, Updated Edition
William Brown

Copyright © 1996 by Hendrickson Publishers, Inc.
P.O. Box 3473
Peabody, Massachusetts 01961-3473

Reprinted from the sixth edition, revised and enlarged, originally entitled
*The Tabernacle and its Priests and Services, Described and Considered in Relation
to Christ and the Church*, published by Oliphant, Anderson & Ferrier, Edinburgh
and London, 1899.

Fourth printing — May 2002

Printed in the United States of America
Hardcover edition: ISBN 1–56563–195–1
Paperback edition: ISBN 1–56563–229–X

CONTENTS

	Page
ILLUSTRATIONS	vii
TABLE OF WEIGHTS AND MEASURES	ix
PREFACE TO THE SIXTH EDITION	xi
CHAPTER 1—INTRODUCTORY	1
CHAPTER 2—THE SILVER FOUNDATION	4
CHAPTER 3—THE GOLDEN WALLS	12
CHAPTER 4—THE CHERUBIM CURTAIN TABERNACLE	24
CHAPTER 5—THE GOAT-HAIR "TENT" (EXOD. 26:14)	28
CHAPTER 6—THE TWO-FOLD SKIN ROOF	32
CHAPTER 7—THE BEAUTIFUL DOORS	34
CHAPTER 8—WITHIN THE CHERUBIM CURTAIN TABERNACLE	36
CHAPTER 9—THE COURT OF GOD'S HOUSE	41
CHAPTER 10—THE BRAZEN ALTAR	48
CHAPTER 11—THE SHINING LAVER	54
CHAPTER 12—THE SHEWBREAD TABLE	58
CHAPTER 13—THE GOLDEN ALTAR	62
CHAPTER 14—THE SEVEN-BRANCHED GOLDEN CANDLESTICK	67
CHAPTER 15—THE ARK OF THE COVENANT	73
CHAPTER 16—THE PRIESTS	85
CHAPTER 17—THE GARMENTS FOR GLORY AND BEAUTY	87
CHAPTER 18—THE LEVITES	113
CHAPTER 19—THE SACRIFICES UNDER THE LAW	118

CHAPTER 20—THE DAILY SERVICE 129

CHAPTER 21—THE GREAT DAY OF ATONEMENT 135

CHAPTER 22—THE SUPERIORITY OF THE HOLY OF HOLIES. 144

CHAPTER 23—THE ENCAMPMENT AND ORDER OF MARCH 151

CHAPTER 24—THE CLOUDY PILLAR. 164

APPENDIX

CHAPTER 25—THE HEBREW CUBIT 181

CHAPTER 26—CONJECTURES AS TO THE BREADTH OF THE HOUSE 186

CHAPTER 27—THE SURPLUSAGE OF THE CHERUBIM AND
GOAT-HAIR CURTAINS. 190

CHAPTER 28—MR. FERGUSSON'S SLOPING ROOF TABERNACLE. 192

CHAPTER 29—THE DEAN OF CANTERBURY AND
PROFESSOR MILLIGAN ON THE TABERNACLE 206

CHAPTER 30—THE PEREGRINATIONS OF THE GOLDEN CANDLESTICK 211

ILLUSTRATIONS

Page

High Priest. . . . . *ii*

FOR THE SILVER FOUNDATION

One Hundred Silver Sockets 5
Dovetailing Sockets 6
One Hundred Flat Sockets. 7

FOR THE GOLDEN WALLS

Board and its Tenons. 12
Conjecture as to Corner Boards and Breadth of House. 13
Five Rows of Bars Variously Arranged 14
Various Modes of Arranging the Bars. 15
Pillar. 16
Diagrams Showing All the Boards, Tenons, Sockets, Bars, Rings,
    and Pillars of the Tabernacle Framework. 17
Prospective View of Tabernacle Framework. 18

FOR CURTAINS AND HANGINGS

Cherub Curtain 25
Two Great Cherubim Curtains of Five Curtains and Loops 26
Ten Cherubim Curtains Indicating How Arranged 27
One Goat-Hair and One Cherub Curtain, Showing Difference in Size . . 28
Two Great Goat-Hair Curtains, One of Five and One of Six Curtains . . . 29
Eleven Goat-Hair Curtains, Indicating How Arranged 30

FOR COURT, FURNITURE, PRIESTS, ETC.

Diagram of Court, Showing Pillars and Hangings, and Positions of
    Altar, Laver, Sanctuary, and Cloudy Pillar. 40
Brazen Altar (No. 1) 48

Brazen Altar (No. 2) 50

Laver (No. 1) 54

Laver (No. 2) 55

Table of Shewbread 58

Golden Altar... 63

Golden Candlestick 66

Bas-Relief from Arch of Titus 68

Candlestick and Bearers, from Photograph of Section of Arch 69

Ark of the Covenant, Mercy Seat, and Cherubim................. 74

Priest (No. 1) 84

High Priest (No. 1) 88

Priest (No. 2) 90

High Priest (No. 2) 94

Diagrams of Names on the Two Stones on Shoulder Pieces 98

Diagram of Names on Breastplate............................. 103

Diagram of Breastplate 104

Lace of Blue for Fixing Golden Crown to the Mitre............... 109

Great Day of Atonement 138

Encampment and Order of March 153

Tabernacle and Court from Beza's Bible (1593) 154

The Court and the Cloudy Pillar.............................. 163

Josephus' Conjecture as to Corner Boards and Breadth of House.... 187

Kalisch's Conjecture as to Corner Boards and Breadth of House 188

Pressland's South-West Corner................................ 188

Gerlach's Conjecture as to Corner Boards and Breadth of House.... 189

Author's Conjecture as to Corner Boards and Breadth of House 190

Ring or Staple for Corner Boards 190

Length of Tabernacle and Sloping Roof, According to Fergusson.... 196

Two Sides of Fergusson's Sloping Roof......................... 196

Cubit hanging over at North and South Sides 197

Perspective View of Mr. Fergusson's Tabernacle Restored......... 197

Diagram Illustrating Sides Westward 200

Open Spaces at Back End and Front, for Which No
    Curtains Are Provided 204

TABLE OF WEIGHTS AND MEASURES ADOPTED IN THIS WORK

3 inches.	. . . .	Make 1 handbreadth
9 inches	. . . .	Make 1 span
18 inches or two spans	. . . .	Make 1 cubit
3000 shekels	. . . .	Make 1 talent
1500 ounces	. . . .	Make 1 talent

On the Length of the Hebrew Cubit, see appendix, chapter 25

Preface to Sixth Edition

The Fifth Edition of this work having been out of print for a considerable time, this New Edition is issued in the hope that the circulation may be still further increased. It has been carefully revised, and for the most part re-written. In order to adapt it better than the previous editions for general readers, critical, technical, and controversial matter have been left out of the book, and formed into an Appendix. Much fresh information is given, amounting to sixty pages, including a chapter on the much disputed subject of the length of the Hebrew Cubit, and another on the wonderful peregrinations of the golden candlestick. The new illustrations include one of a priest and one of a high priest attired in their robes of office, in conformity to the Hebrew text, taken from my life-size model of the high priest. A glance at the Table of Contents and the List of Illustrations will show the plan of the work.

W.B.

1
Introductory

"Let them make Me a Sanctuary."

The tabernacle, made with hands, was devised by the Lord Himself, who showed the "fashion" of it to Moses on Mount Sinai, at the same time strictly enjoining him to see that all things were made according to this divine "pattern" (Exod. 25:9, 40; 26:30; 27:8, Heb. 8:5). The Lord also chose the chief artists under whose superintendence it was to be constructed (Exod. 31:1–6). Are not these circumstances alone sufficient to invest the sacred building with an abiding interest? As a work of art, it was far more beautiful and costly than many persons are apt to suppose.

Make this tabernacle and all its furnishings exactly like the pattern I will show you (Exod. 25:9).

Even Dean Stanley, in the second series of his "Lectures on the Jewish Church," at p. 227, says: "There is no inherent connection between 'ugliness' and 'holiness,' and there was a greater danger of superstition in the 'rough planks' and 'black haircloths' of the tabernacle than ever was in the gilded walls and marble towers of the temple."

No one unacquainted with the Bible description of the tabernacle, on reading these words of the late Dean, would ever imagine that the foundation of this sacred structure was formed of solid silver; that the "planks" composing its sides were all *very smooth*, and, moreover, gilded with gold; that its pillars were graceful and adorned with capitals; that even the capitals of the pillars of the surrounding court and their connecting rods were overlaid with silver; and that

They serve at a sanctuary that is a copy and shadow of what is in heaven. This is why Moses was warned when he was about to build the tabernacle: "See to it that you make everything according to the pattern shown you on the mountain" (Heb. 8:5).

the goat-hair curtains, even granting they were black (though most writers are of opinion that they were manufactured of fine, white, soft, silky hair, similar to that of the Angora goat), were draped with the most brilliant and gorgeous tapestry, into which figures of cherubim were beautifully interwoven. There certainly was no roughness or coarseness or ugliness either within or without. The structure was worthy of its divine architect; honoring to the willing-hearted Israelites, who gave two hundred and fifty thousand pounds sterling worth of gifts for its construction; and creditable to the many skilled artisans who vied with each other in carrying out the design of their God and King.

There are not a few, who, like the late Dean Stanley, have a very inadequate idea of the tabernacle, and who, without studying the subject, but trusting to what he and some others say, or to their own imagination, both in speech and writing belittle this portable temple. To him and them the splendors and glory of Solomon's and Herod's temples so loom in their view as to all but eclipse the poor tabernacle. Not so was it treated by the inspired author of the Hebrews; he passed by these two grand and world-wide celebrated temples as if of no consequence in comparison with their great antitype the tabernacle, on which he fixes his attention and regard. It is of it he speaks, of its holy places, of its golden vessels, of its veil, of its ark and overarching cherubim, of its ministering servants, of its priests, of its high priest, of its services and sacrifices—it is of these that he discourses and eloquently and effectively shows their typical and spiritual significance.

Though it is not right in every case to judge of the importance of a Bible subject by the space it occupies in Holy Writ, yet it may not be unworthy of remark that much more is said about the tabernacle than about Solomon's temple, both in the Old Testament and in the New. Nearly three hundred verses in Exodus are devoted to an account of the tabernacle and its furniture, while the corresponding account of the temple and its furniture, in First Kings and Second Chronicles, is comprised in half that number of verses.

The tabernacle, its priests, its rites, and its sacrifices have all passed away, but the description and history of them remain, and form part of those sacred writings which testify of Christ, who said of Moses, "He wrote of Me."

Many of the most important words and phrases employed in the New Testament have either arisen from, or are illustrated by, the tabernacle and its rites, of which the following are examples:—"Veil," "Mercy seat," "Propitiation," "Laver of Regeneration," "Lamb of God who taketh away the sin of the world," "Washed," "Cleansed," "Purged," "Reconciled," "Sacrifice," "Offering," "Atonement," "Without shedding of blood is no remission," "Gave Himself for us," "Bore our sins in His own body on the tree."

The pages of Exodus, our text-book of the tabernacle, are all gilded with the rays of the Sun of Righteousness. Exodus is the most picturesque book of the Bible. It contains more word-pictures than any other. And they can all be turned into real pictures, a task which in a rough way we have tried to perform with many of them in order to illustrate our book. Those connected with our subject portray features of Him who is altogether lovely. They all speak of Him, they all sing His praise, and they all unite in the one loud, grand, and ever resounding chorus, "Christ is all and in all."

An earnest and prayerful study of the tabernacle, and the purposes it served, cannot fail to increase our knowledge of the grand truths of redemption. That you may find the following chapters in some degree interesting, and derive some profit from their perusal, and may, while studying this earthly sanctuary, be growing in meekness for the heavenly and its unutterable joys, is the prayer of your friend the author. May David's choice be yours: "One thing I desired of the Lord, that will I seek after; that I may dwell in the house of the Lord all the days of my life, to behold the beauty of the Lord, and to inquire in His temple."

Then the LORD said to Moses, "See, I have chosen Bezalel son of Uri, the son of Hur, of the tribe of Judah, and I have filled him with the Spirit of God, with skill, ability and knowledge in all kinds of crafts-to make artistic designs for work in gold, silver and bronze, to cut and set stones, to work in wood, and to engage in all kinds of craftsmanship" (Exod. 31:1–5).

Silver = Redemption

2
THE SILVER FOUNDATION

God promised to take up His abode in the midst of His people Israel, provided they gave Him a beautiful and costly palace-temple for a dwelling, made of gold, silver and other suitable material (Exod. 25:1–7), and constructed entirely according to His own design (Exod. 26:30; Acts 7:44; Heb. 8:5)—"Let them make Me a sanctuary that I may dwell among them" (Exod. 25:8). They agreed, and built the sacred edifice (Exod. 36; 37; 38).

The Foundation consisted of one hundred blocks of silver, called sockets (26:19–25; 38:27), arranged as follows:—forty along the south side (Exod. 26:18, 19); forty along the north side (vv. 20, 21); sixteen along the west side (v. 25), and four across the house (vv. 31, 32): in all one hundred. In the diagram on the next page the blocks of silver are all numbered and the place each occupied in the foundation indicated by dots. Sockets 41 and 42, and sockets 55 and 56 being for the corners are so shaped and placed as to suit the corner boards resting on them. See diagram, p. 7.

Union of the sockets.—When placed in rows on the ground to form the foundation, the sockets required to be joined to each other in some way, and most likely this was done by the simple method of dovetailing, as shown in the illustration.

By this means each socket was able to go into and take hold of its neighbor: number 2 going into and taking hold of number 1; number 3 going into and taking hold of number 2; and number 4 into

THE ONE HUNDRED SILVER SOCKETS.

42 43 44 45 46 47 48 49 50 51 52 53 54 55

Nos 41, 42, 55, 56, are the sockets for the corner boards.
The dots intended to represent the position of the centre of the sockets.

40 at each of the long sides, 16 at the back end (which includes the 4 for the corner boards), and the 4 for the pillars which divided the Holy Place from the Holy of Holies.

97   98   99   100

Set up the tabernacle according to the plan shown you on the mountain (Exod. 26:30).

number 3, and so on all the way round. Each joining to each and all to each, they formed a basis sufficiently strong to bear up the three golden walls of the tabernacle.

Length and Breadth of the House Determined by the Length of the Sockets

It is generally agreed that the tabernacle was 30 cubits long and 10 broad. To form a continuous base of silver under the three walls of a building of the

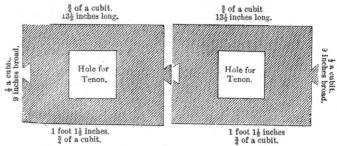

*Face or upper side of two Sockets constructed so as to dovetail
into each other. Scale—2 inches to a cubit.*
FROM MODEL TABERNACLE.

*The 100 talents of silver
were used to cast the bases
for the sanctuary and for
the curtain—100 bases
from the 100 talents, one
talent for each base
(Exod. 38:27).*

above dimension, it was necessary that each socket should be three-quarters of a cubit long. The size of the sockets is not given in the Scriptures; but as the length of two sockets was equal to the breadth of the board (1½ cubits) which rested on them (Exod. 26:16 with 19), it follows that a socket as required was three-quarters of a cubit long. Each socket weighted a talent (Exod. 38:27), equal to 1500 ounces or 93¾ lbs. This quantity of silver is sufficient to form a socket of the above length, and half a cubit broad and a quarter of a cubit deep (see illustration above). We submitted our calculation to a practical silversmith, who measured and then weighed our sockets in his fine scales, and they were not found wanting.

The length of forty sockets (the number at each long side of the house), each three-quarters of a cubit long, is 30 cubits, being the length of the tabernacle. The length of twelve of the back or west side sockets (43 to 54 inclusive), each three-quarters of a cubit long, is 9 cubits, one short of the breadth. The additional cubit is obtained as follows:—Half of socket 42, and half of socket 55, are included in the breadth of the interior of the house, as the back of diagram (p. 7) shows. Together, the two halves measure three-quarters of a cubit, which, added to the above nine cubits, make nine and three-quarter cubits. The breadth of the house extends from the south margin of the socket holes on the one side of the house to the north margin of the socket holes on the other side of the house. The space between said margin and the

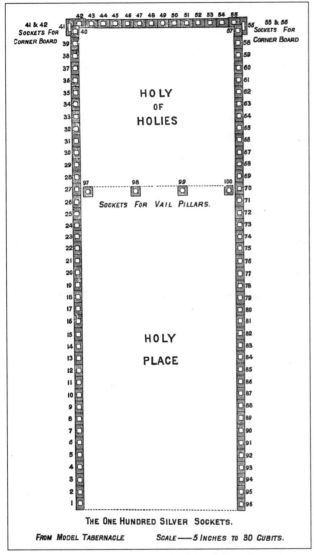

The above diagram is 108th of the size of the Tabernacle.
Thirty cubits is equal to one hundred and eight inches.

edge of the sockets, one-eighth of a cubit (see diagram above) on each side of the house, together one-quarter of a cubit, falls to be added to the above nine and three-quarter cubits, and thus gives ten cubits (15 feet) as the internal breadth of the tabernacle as required.

Diagram of the One Hundred Silver Sockets, and the Size of the Tabernacle

The 100 talents of silver were used to cast the bases for the sanctuary and for the curtain—100 bases from the 100 talents, one talent for each base (Exod. 38:27).

The illustration of the hundred sockets on p. 7, on the scale of one-sixth of an inch to a cubit, or of 5 inches to 30 cubits, will be found very nearly correct—we say nearly, for the woodcut block has shrunk to the extent of about one-sixteenth of an inch in the process of electrotyping. For the internal breadth of the house and its apartments, measure from the inside margin of the socket holes on the south side to the inside margin of those on the north side; for its length, measure from the inside margin of the socket holes at the back end to the dotted lines at the entrance of the tabernacle. For the length of the holy of holies, measure from the inside margin of the socket holes at the back end to the dotted line, which indicates the threshold of this apartment; and for the length of the holy place, measure from the one dotted line to the other, and the woodcut measurement will be found to be:—

Tabernacle,. . . . . 30 sixths of an inch by 10 sixths.
Holy Place, ... 20 sixths of an inch by 10 sixths.
Holy of Holies, ... 10 sixths of an inch by 10 sixths.

As the tabernacle was 108 times the size of the woodcut, by multiplying each of the above measurements by 108, the product will be found to agree with the actual internal size of the tabernacle and its apartments:—

Tabernacle,. . . . . 30 cubits by 10 cubits, or 45 feet by 15 feet.
Holy Place, ... 20 cubits by 10 cubits, or 30 feet by 15 feet.
Holy of Holies, ... 10 cubits by 10 cubits, or 15 feet by 15 feet.

The diagram of the hundred silver sockets (p. 7) shows the ground-plan of the building to consist, like that of the temple, of two apartments; the outer one, the holy place, a double square, 20 cubits by 10, and the inner one, the holy of holies, a perfect square, 10 cubits by 10. The temple was exactly double the size of the tabernacle.

Value of the sockets.—Each socket weighed a talent (Exod. 38:27), equal to 1500 oz., worth, when the silver was raised for the foundation, at least £400, so that the value of the hundred was not less than £40,000.

Raising of the silver.—Shortly before the time we are speaking of, God delivered His people out of the hands of their cruel enemies the Egyptians, whom He caused to be drowned in the Red Sea. In consequence, He claimed the Israelite men, whose lives He saved, as His, allowing them, however, with the exception of the Levites retained in His sacred service (Num. 1:47–50; 3:11–16, 40, 41), to redeem themselves by paying Him a price, so that they might be free to attend to their own and their family affairs. The price—a very small one, to enable every man to give it—was a silver coin, a little larger than our shilling, called a half-shekel (Exod. 30:13), and worth 1s. 3d. in our money.

But Moses said to God, "Who am I, that I should go to Pharaoh and bring the Israelites out of Egypt?" And God said, "I will be with you. And this will be the sign to you that it is I who have sent you: When you have brought the people out of Egypt, you will worship God on this mountain" (Exod. 3:11–12).

When all the pretty glittering coins were counted, it was found they numbered 603,350, being the same as the number of the men (Num. 1:46), showing that every man paid his ransom money. The 603,350 half shekels, divided by 6000, the number of half shekels in a talent, show that the total amount in talents was 100 talents, and 1775 shekels (or seven-twelfths of a talent). This summation exactly agrees with that of the sacred historian (Exod. 38:25).

Of the hundred talents of silver were cast the one hundred sockets, forming the foundation of the tabernacle (Exod. 27:27). The fraction of seven-twelfths of a talent we wish you not to forget. As we shall see by-and-by, it was used for upholding the court wall, so that both sanctuary and court were upheld by the atonement money, a circumstance worthy of notice (see chapter 9, p. 41).

Christ And Redemption

The redemption of sinners in some respects is like that of the Israelite men, and in some respects quite different. As God estimated every Israelite man at the same value, and on that account required every one to pay the like price for his ransom—"the rich were not to give more, and the poor were not to give less" (Exod. 30:15)—so He estimates every sinner at the same value, and consequently requires the same price to be paid for every one, for the beggar as well as for the king, for the least as well as for the greatest sinner. Such, however, is the nature of what sinners need to be redeemed from (Gal. 3:13), and such the nature of the soul, that no mere nominal price, as that in the case of the Israelite men, or any price, however great, a sinner might be capable of giving, can suffice to satisfy the law's demands or those of the holy and righteous lawgiver.

Christ redeemed us from the curse of the law by becoming a curse for us, for it is written: "Cursed is everyone who is hung on a tree" (Gal. 3:13).

Behind the multitude of faces we meet in our crowded streets and elsewhere, there glitters, though defaced by sin, a priceless gem, an immortal soul which nothing earthly, not even the great globe we inhabit and all that it contains, can redeem—nothing can, save the price paid by Him who loved us and gave Himself for us: "Ye are redeemed not with corruptible things, as silver and gold, . . . but with the precious blood of Christ (1 Peter 1:18).

When the Israelite man paid his ransom, he became, as we have seen, in a sense his own property; but those who by faith have become sharers in the blessings of redemption, have ceased to be their own property and become that of their Redeemer; "ye are not your own, for ye are bought with a price; therefore glorify God in your body, and in your spirit, which are God's" (1 Cor. 6:19, 20).

Christ the Church's Sure Foundation

The beautiful shining foundation made of the ransom silver, worth forty thousand pounds sterling, constituted a very costly basis, from which our thoughts not unnaturally rise to an infinitely more valuable one, even to Him "who gave Himself a ransom for all." Prophets and apostles alike testify that He is the sure foundation on which the spiritual edifice rests. Had the sockets not been made of the atonement money as commanded (Exod. 30:16; 38:27), but of some other material, God certainly would not have acknowledged the tabernacle as His palace-temple. He never would have enthroned Himself in visible symbol on the mercy seat. In like manner, those who substitute their own good works, or anything else, in the room of the Redeemer, on which to build their hope of salvation, are building on the sand, and cannot form a part of that building which is an "habitation of God through the Spirit," for "other foundation can no man lay than is laid, which is Christ Jesus." Rest, then, on Him, and on Him alone, and your hope will be founded on Rock that will never fail you, and you will be one of the living stones of the great spiritual temple, and He who dwelt between the cherubim will dwell in you, and be your God.

Receive the atonement money from the Israelites and use it for the service of the Tent of Meeting. It will be a memorial for the Israelites before the LORD, making atonement for your lives (Exod. 30:16).

> I stand upon His merit,
>   I know no other stand;
> Not e'en where glory dwelleth
>   In Immanuel's land.

3
THE GOLDEN WALLS

Each frame is to be ten cubits long and a cubit and a half wide (Exod. 26:16).

We now go on to build the gold house, and, as divinely directed on the silver foundation we have been laying.

The Forty-Eight Gold Covered Boards

Of these, twenty stood on the south side (Exod. 26:18), twenty on the north (v. 20); six with two corner ones on the west (vv. 22–25). In all forty-eight. Each measured 10 cubits high, and $1^1/_2$ cubits broad (v. 16).

Length and Breadth of the House, Determined by the Breadth of the Boards

By multiplying 20, the number of the boards at each long side, by $1^1/_2$ cubits, the breadth of a board, we get the exact length of the house, 30 cubits; but by multiplying the six west end boards by $1^1/_2$ cubits, we get only 9 cubits, one too few for the breadth of the house, and if we include the two corner boards, we get 12 cubits, two too many. By making the two corner boards angular in shape as their name suggests, each consisting of two equal halves of an ordinary board, dovetailed or otherwise united, yet so that when united they constitute but one board; one half of each of these corner boards facing the back end, and the other half of each facing respectively the south and north sides, we get the required breadth of the house, 10 cubits (diagram, p. 13). See further with respect to corner boards and breadth of the house, appendix, chapter 26.

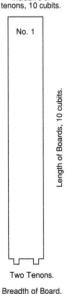

Board to rest on sockets placed on the ground; length of board inclusive of tenons, 10 cubits.

No. 1

Length of Boards, 10 cubits.

Two Tenons.

Breadth of Board, $1^1/_2$ cubits.

FROM MODEL TABERNACLE.

The length of the socket, $^3/_4$ of a cubit (p. 6), and the breadth of the board, $1^1/_2$ cubits (p. 12), both combine to show that the internal length of the house was 30 cubits (45 feet), and the breadth 10 cubits (15 feet). The size of the curtains also shows that the house was of these dimensions. See chapter 4, "On the Cherubim Curtains."

The Bars

Five gold covered bars went along the sides of the tabernacle (Exod. 26:26–29). Four of the bars, as shown in our specimen board (p. 14), passed through gold rings fixed to each board. The third, or middle bar, however, did not pass through rings (v. 28), but through the boards themselves, a hole being bored through them for the purpose as indicated in the illustration (p. 14). "He made the middle bar to shoot through the boards from the one end to the other" (Exod. 36:33).

The general opinion is that there were five bars to each of three sides arranged in so many rows—the middle one reaching the whole length, while the other four ran along only part of the wall. See woodcut No. 1, p. 15.

Some are of opinion that the five bars formed three rows, the four shorter ones running half the distance—two at or near the foot, and starting from each end, and meeting at the middle of the boards; and two near the top, similarly arranged—the middle bar running the whole distance (see No. 2, p. 15). The objection to this conjecture is, that no sufficient reason can be shown why, if the middle row should consist of but one bar, the other two rows should consist of two bars each.

No. 3 (p. 15) shows the four short bars transversing the sides, as some think they should, and meeting in the center of the wall, and the middle one reaching from end to end. This may seem to agree with the text, but it removes the bars from the foot and the top of the boards while the top especially may be supposed to require a bar.

Also make crossbars of acacia wood: five for the frames on one side of the tabernacle, five for those on the other side, and five for the frames on the west, at the far end of the tabernacle. The center crossbar is to extend from end to end at the middle of the frames. Overlay the frames with gold and make gold rings to hold the crossbars. Also overlay the crossbars with gold (Exod. 26:26–29).

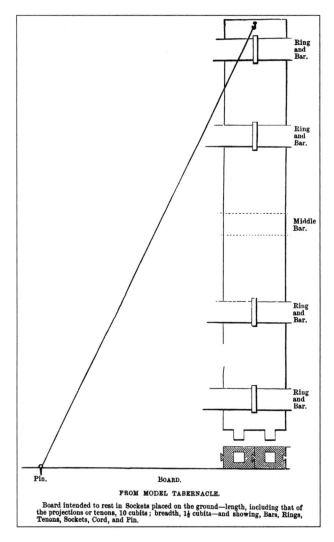

FROM MODEL TABERNACLE.

Board intended to rest in Sockets placed on the ground—length, including that of the projections or tenons, 10 cubits ; breadth, 1½ cubits—and showing, Bars, Rings, Tenons, Sockets, Cord, and Pin.

No. 4 (p. 15) is intended to represent the middle bar as passing through the heart of the boards, which have been mortised for this purpose to admit of its passing through them. The other four bars run along the outside. We do not think the text implies that the four bars ran along only part of the wall, but that the middle bar entered in at the one end of the wall, and, passing through the heart or inside of the boards, reached to the other end, and that the other four bars extended along the walls on the outside. This view appears to be in harmony with the text, "And he

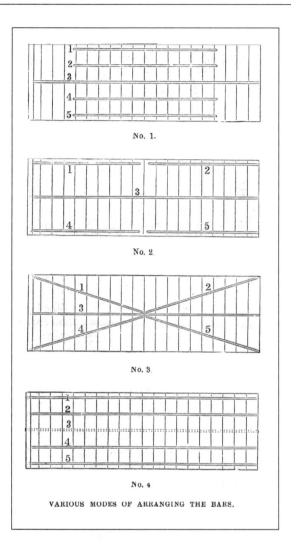

No. 1.

No. 2.

No. 3.

No. 4.

VARIOUS MODES OF ARRANGING THE BARS.

made the middle bar to shoot through the boards from the one end to the other" (Exod. 36:33).

The woodcut on p. 14 will fully illustrate a tabernacle board in connection with its tenons, sockets, bars, rings, cord, and pin. .

The Tenons

At the foot of every board, as shown in the illustration at p. 14, were two tenons (Heb. "hands"), by means of these each board went into and took hold of its two ransom silver sockets, and as the boards thus

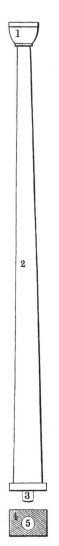

FROM MODEL.

1. Capital. 2. Shaft.
3. Tenon. 4. Socket.
5. Hole for Tenon.

by their hands went into their respective sockets, the sockets in their turn took hold of the boards by a firm grip and upheld them. The cord and pin shown in our specimen board will be noticed afterward.

Pillars

Four pillars overlaid with gold and resting on silver sockets, stood at the distance of 20 cubits from the entrance to the sacred dwelling, and 10 cubits from the back wall (see woodcut, p. 17). Five similar pillars stood at the entrance of the tabernacle (p. 17). It may appear singular to some that their sockets were not made of ransom silver, like those of the four pillars and those of the golden boards. The reason is that they (the sockets for the five pillars) were situated immediately on the outside of the threshold of the house, and on that account, being considered as pertaining to the court and not to the sanctuary, were, like the rest of the court sockets, made of brass. (See threshold indicated in diagram, p. 7.)

View of All the Parts
of the Golden Frame-Work

The silver sockets, comprising the foundation of the tabernacle, and the various parts comprising the golden frame-work, having been illustrated in detail, a kind of bird's eye view of the whole is given on p. 17 by means of diagrams. The three walls are supposed to be raised from their foundations and laid flat on their sides, enabling you to see all the boards, bars, tenons, rings, and staples. The sockets, represented by dots, describe the ground-plan. In imagination raise the three walls, bring them to the ground-plan, place the tenons in their respective sockets, and rear up the pillars, and the eye of your mind will have presented to it a model of the gold and silver edifice. The illustration on p. 18 is a perspective view taken from our model of the sacred structure.

In this view all the sockets, boards, rings, bars, and pillars are represented. Twenty boards at the south side are shown standing in and on their forty sockets; twenty at the north side, standing in and on

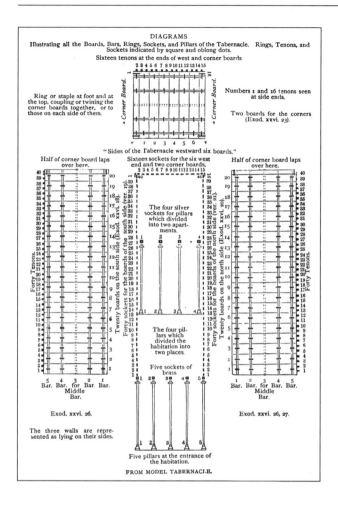

DIAGRAMS

Illustrating all the Boards, Bars, Rings, Sockets, and Pillars of the Tabernacle. Rings, Tenons, and Sockets indicated by square and oblong dots.

Sixteen tenons at the ends of west and corner boards

Ring or staple at foot and at the top, coupling or twining the corner boards together, or to those on each side of them.

Numbers 1 and 16 tenons seen at side ends.

Two boards for the corners (Exod. xxvi. 23).

"Sides of the Tabernacle westward six boards."

Half of corner board laps over here.

Sixteen sockets for the six west end and two corner boards.

Half of corner board laps over here.

The four silver sockets for pillars which divided into two apartments.

The four pillars which divided the habitation into two places.

Five sockets of brass

5 4 3 2 1
Bar. Bar. for Bar. Bar.
Middle
Bar.

Exod. xxvi. 26.

1 2 3 4 5
Bar. Bar. for Bar. Bar.
Middle
Bar.

Exod. xxvi. 26, 27.

The three walls are represented as lying on their sides.

Five pillars at the entrance of the habitation.

FROM MODEL TABERNACLE.

their forty sockets; six with two corner boards at the back end, standing in and on their sixteen sockets; and four pillars within the house, standing in and on their four sockets—in all, forty-eight gold-covered boards and four gold-covered pillars, standing in and on the one hundred atonement silver money sockets (Exod. 38:27). Four rows of bars passing through gold rings extend along the three sides of the house, clasping firmly board to board; the boards being still more closely knit together by means of the middle bar, an unseen yet strong uniting and supporting band acting like a backbone to the structure, while the outside bars act like ribs. The building is still further compacted by means of the corner boards and

Also make crossbars of acacia wood: five for the frames on one side of the tabernacle, five for those on the other side, and five for the frames on the west, at the far end of the tabernacle (Exod. 26:26, 27).

From Model.　Framework of Tabernacle.

corner sockets, uniting the three walls into one whole. The five gold-covered pillars resting on their five brazen sockets stand like guardian angels before the entrance to the sanctuary.

Thus at the foot of Mount Sinai the many and divers parts of the sacred building were made, and without a single nail or noise of hammer fitly framed into one beautiful compact gold and silver tabernacle, and so constructed as to be easily taken to pieces and easily rebuilt again, this being necessary, as frequently it had to be removed from one place to another in the wilderness. When finished with its cherubim and other curtains, hangings and coverings, and surrounded by its lovely court, it was the most costly and magnificent portable temple ever made with hands. As a work of art it was complete, lacking in nothing. All this need not greatly surprise you, for its Architect was He of whom it is said in the Bible, "His work is perfect," and who inspired the master builders, Bezaleel and Aholiab, and other craftsmen, with wisdom (Exod. 36:1) for their great undertaking, strictly charging Moses to see that all things were made according to the pattern which, while enshrined with Him in the cloud of glory on Mount

So Bezalel, Oholiab and every skilled person to whom the LORD has given skill and ability to know how to carry out all the work of constructing the sanctuary are to do the work just as the LORD has commanded (Exod. 36:1).

Sinai, He caused to pass before His servant's wondering and admiring eyes.

£3000 worth of gold was used in covering one board, and in covering them all £144,000. The entire gold offering weighed 29 talents and 730 shekels (Exod. 38:24), equal to 43,865 ounces. Approximate value of gifts for the tabernacle:—

The Gold Offering

	£	s	d
Gold 43,865 oz. At £4, 4s. Per oz.,	184,233	0	0
Silver 150,887½ oz., at 2s. 4d. Per oz.,	17,603	10	10
Brass (or Copper) 106,200 oz., at ³/₄d. Per oz.,	331	17	6
Say for probable higher price of the precious metals at the time of the Exodus,	50,000	0	0
	£252,168	8	4

And if you add to this the value of the voluntary offerings of other needful materials used in the construction of the building, and the value of the workmanship freely executed by the Israelites, who lent their hands as well as gave their gifts, £300,000 may not be too high a sum at which to value the tabernacle. Even this large sum, however, does not fully indicate the liberality of the Hebrew pilgrims, for we do not know how much more they might have brought, had they not "been restrained from bringing, for the stuff they had was sufficient for all the work to make it, and too much" (Exod. 36:6, 7).

Then Moses gave an order and they sent this word throughout the camp: "No man or woman is to make anything else as an offering for the sanctuary." And so the people were restrained from bringing more, because what they already had was more than enough to do all the work (Exod. 36:6–7).

Only men were allowed to bring silver, and neither less nor more than half a shekel each; but all, men and women alike, were invited to bring other material, and as much as they were able or inclined to fetch. Gold was brought in the form of bracelets, ear-rings, seal-rings, and tablets (or necklaces). Those not able to bring gold, brought brass, wood, flax, linen, goat-hair, skins, and other needful materials.

Every jewel brought, as well as every other gift, great or small, bore a beautiful stamp, heaven's hall mark, a willing heart. It was this willing-heartedness that spiritualized and transfigured the free-will offerings, and which causes them to shine with imperishable luster on the beautiful pages of Exodus for our edification and imitation.

New Testament Israelites are invited to bring gifts for the building of a greater temple than the tabernacle, and that all may enjoy the privilege of giving, the very smallest offerings are acceptable. As the hair and the skins brought by some who may not have had jewels to bestow were as necessary for the construction of the sacred structure as the more costly offerings of their richer brethren, so the coppers of the poor, or of little children, are as needful to assist in building the spiritual edifice as the sovereigns of the wealthy. The immense service rendered by pence in spreading the Redeemer's kingdom is beyond all human calculation. Pence only, however, will not be an acceptable offering from those who have the more precious metals at their disposal. Gold and silver, as well as brass or copper, were among the materials with which the tabernacle was constructed, and they are also required for building up the church of God. If you have these, and would follow the example of the Hebrew givers, you will not keep them back. If the poor bring pence, see that you forget not to lay silver and gold on the altar. One thing in particular the Lord asks you to give. Refuse it, and your offerings, however costly, will be discarded by Him as nought; but give Him this one thing, and then, as in the case of the Hebrew givers, all else He would like you to bring will crowd after it, and be heaped along with it on the gospel altar. "Son, daughter, give me thine heart." God had recently done great things for Israel, and no doubt a sense of gratitude prompted their liberality; but He has done greater things for both Jews and gentiles: "He so loved the world that He gave His only-begotten Son, that whosoever believeth in Him should not perish, but have everlasting life;" and Jesus "gave Himself for us, that He might redeem us from all iniquity, and purify unto Himself a peculiar people."

Give generously to him and do so without a grudging heart; then because of this the LORD your God will bless you in all your work and in everything you put your hand to (Deut. 15:10).

I gave my life for thee,
  My precious blood I shed,
That thou might'st ransomed be,
  And quickened from the dead.
I gave my life for thee;
What hast thou given for Me?

Be not content with mere giving, be girt for service.
There is work enough in the Christian church not
only for Bezaleels and Aholiabs—for ministers,
elders, and missionaries—but for all Christ's disciples. None are so unifluential but they may do something for the Master's cause. If not in teaching little
children the sweet name of Jesus, or in visiting the
abodes of the godless, or in handing tracts to this and
that person as opportunity offers, yet in one or other
of the endless ways in which they may engage in
works of faith and labors of love. How many alas!
who bear Christ's name stand listlessly by, and refuse
to give heed to the Master's voice, "Why stand ye here
all the day idle?"

If professing Christians were to give as liberally
as the Hebrews gave for the work of the tabernacle,
the coffers of the church would soon so overflow as to
necessitate a proclamation from every pulpit in
Christendom commanding the people to bring no
more gifts; and were all who are able for any work
about Zion to come and do it, the laborers would no
longer be few, but many, and sufficiently numerous
as instruments for the conversion of the whole world.
How speedily, then, would Zion's walls be built up,
and the great temple of living stones completed! Do
you long for this glorious consummation? If you do,
see that you delay it not, either by not giving as the
Lord hath prospered you, or by sitting with folded
hands while you should be up and working. And,
dear friend, if you have put your hand to this blessed
employment, let your resolution be that of one of the
noblest builders of old, "I am doing a great work, so
that I cannot come down" (Neh. 6:3).

Laziness brings on deep sleep, and the shiftless man goes hungry (Prov. 19:15).

Analogy between Parts
of the Tabernacle and the Members
of the Spiritual Temple

Him who overcomes I will make a pillar in the temple of my God. Never again will he leave it. I will write on him the name of my God and the name of the city of my God, the new Jerusalem, which is coming down out of heaven from my God; and I will also write on him my new name (Rev. 3:12).

The gold gilded boards.—How lovely the boards must have shone as they stood on the ransom silver, but all who are resting on Jesus their Redeemer shine far more gloriously: they shine with the unfading beauty of holiness.

Tenons and sockets.—At the foot of every board were two tenons or hands (p. 14), to enable it to go into and take hold of its two atonement money sockets, and as the boards by their hands took hold of the ransom silver, the sockets in their turn took hold of the boards with a firm grip and upheld them. Faith is like the board hands, for it is by faith we lay hold of Christ our ransom, and as we lay hold of Him, even though our faith may be feeble, He at the same time, ransom-socket like, lays hold of us with a firm, yea, with an almighty grasp, and will never suffer anyone to pluck us out of His hands.

> Stranger, pilgrim here below,
>   Traveling to fair Canaan's Land,
> Lean on Jesus as you go,
>   For by faith alone ye stand.

Golden bars encircled the boards, and helped, along with the silver foundation, to bear them up and keep them from falling, and so all who are resting on and cleaving to Jesus are surrounded by strong supporting bands, for, as the golden bars around the sacred tent, the everlasting arms are around all God's dear children, so that they can never fall.

Pillars are elegant parts of a structure. They are graceful and yet strong supports. Those of the tabernacle helped to sustain the roof, and the veils were suspended from them. Eminent saints are said to be pillars in the house of God (Rev. 3:12), for they are her ornaments and chief props. With few exceptions, those who enlist early in the Master's service become her brightest ornaments.

If you know that your hopes of heaven and everlasting blessedness rest on the one sure foundation; if you feel the loving arms of your Heavenly Father encircling you, and if, in some degree, you are shining with the beauty of holiness, forget not that you owe all to Him who loved you and gave Himself for you. May the love of Christ, therefore, constrain you to live not unto yourselves, but unto Him who died for you. May there be such evidence of your being united by faith to Christ, the sure foundation, that it may be said of you, "Now therefore ye are no more strangers and foreigners, but fellowcitizens with the saints, and of the household of God; and are built upon the foundation of the apostles and prophets, Jesus Christ Himself being the chief corner stone; in whom all the building fitly framed together groweth into an holy temple in the Lord: in whom ye also are builded together for an habitation of God through the Spirit" (Eph. 2:19–22).

4
THE CHERUBIM CURTAIN TABERNACLE

The curtains, skins, and boards of the sacred edifice, considered as a whole, are called the tabernacle (Heb. "dwelling"), but regarded separately, the cherubim curtains are so named, and consequently in the text (Exod. 36:1–15) have the place of honor, being first mentioned in the order of relative importance thus: first, the cherubim curtains (v. 1); second, the goat-hair curtains (v. 7); third, the two sets of skin coverings (v. 14); and fourth and last, the boards, which are not called the tabernacle (or dwelling), but merely the boards for the tabernacle (v. 1 with vv. 6, 15). The beautiful ornamental cherubim curtains were visible on the roof and walls of the interior, being with their goats' hair tent covering suspended within the house from the top of the boards. There is no other possible sense in which they could have been designated the tabernacle. Some writers throw them over the framework of golden boards, and then cover them entirely over with the goat-hair curtains and the two sets of skin coverings, but certainly two-thirds of the beautiful and highly decorated curtains were never thus intended to be covered and hid from view. Rich tapestry is not used on the outside of buildings, but displayed in the interior. According to the above writers, the cherubim curtains were only displayed to view on the ceiling, and the rest of them unseen.

Made of undyed and dyed linen yarn.—The warp or foundation was of the very finest pure white linen yarn (Heb. "shesh"), and the weft of the same material dyed blue, purple, and scarlet (v. 1). Figures

All the skilled men among the workmen made the tabernacle with ten curtains of finely twisted linen and blue, purple and scarlet yarn, with cherubim worked into them by a skilled craftsman (Exod. 36:8).

of cherubim were interwoven by skillful weavers (v. 1).

The wise-hearted women were the spinners (Exod. 35:25; 35:35).

Some render "shesh" silk (Variorum Bible, mar., Exod. 25), but they are certainly mistaken, for in ancient times the Egyptians used only linen and cotton. It was not till a few centuries before our era that the use of wool and silk . . . was introduced. Egyptian linen was exceedingly fine: Herodotus, describing the breastplate sent to the Lacedæmonians by King Amasis, tells us it was made of linen . . . Each slender thread was composed of three hundred and sixty distinct threads (See Eugene Muntz, *Short History of Tapestry*, pp. 5, 6).

Every skilled woman spun with her hands and brought what she had spun-blue, purple or scarlet yarn or fine linen (Exod. 35:25).

The number and size of the curtains.—There were ten of these very fine and rich curtains woven. Each measured 28 cubits long and 4 broad.

The joining of the curtains.—Five of the curtains were "coupled one to another," and the other five in like manner (Exod. 26:3) probably by needlework, forming two great curtains joined together by means of loops of blue and taches of gold (vv. 4, 6); fifty loops extending along the outermost edge of one of the great curtains, and fifty along that of the other (vv. 4, 5). At the place where the junction was effected, loops took hold one of the other, and were kept locked together by means of the golden clasps (v. 6). (See diagram of the two great cherubim curtains, p. 26.)

Join five of the curtains together, and do the same with the other five (Exod. 26:3).

Disposition of the curtains.—The curtains were placed lengthways across the roof, and down the side

FROM MODEL TABERNACLE.

Fine Linen or Cherub Curtain, 28 cubits long.

Scale—⅒th of an inch to a cubit.

walls; but as the wall on each side was 10 cubits high, and the roof 10 cubits broad (in all 30 cubits), and as the curtains were only 28 cubits long, they did not quite reach to the ground, but to a cubit of it on both sides. (See diagram, p. 28.)

Length and Breadth of the House Determined by the Size of the Curtains

(See diagram, p. 27.)

Join five of the curtains together, and do the same with the other five. Make loops of blue material along the edge of the end curtain in one set, and do the same with the end curtain in the other set. Make fifty loops on one curtain and fifty loops on the end curtain of the other set, with the loops opposite each other (Exod. 26:3–5).

The breadth of the first grand division of five curtains being twenty cubits extended along the roof of the holy place (See diagram), and ten cubits of the second grand division of twenty cubits, extended along the roof of the most holy place, showing that the combined length of the two apartments was thirty cubits, the remaining ten cubits of this grand division hung down the back wall. That the two great curtains

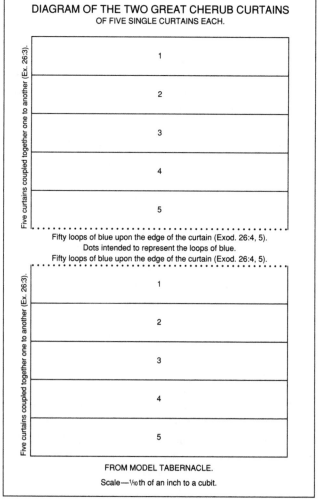

DIAGRAM OF THE TWO GREAT CHERUB CURTAINS
OF FIVE SINGLE CURTAINS EACH.

Five curtains coupled together one to another (Ex. 26:3).

1

2

3

4

5

Fifty loops of blue upon the edge of the curtain (Exod. 26:4, 5).
Dots intended to represent the loops of blue.
Fifty loops of blue upon the edge of the curtain (Exod. 26:4, 5).

Five curtains coupled together one to another (Ex. 26:3).

1

2

3

4

5

FROM MODEL TABERNACLE.
Scale—1/10th of an inch to a cubit.

DIAGRAM OF THE TEN CHERUB CURTAINS, Showing how much was required to cover the walls and ceiling of the Tabernacle, and how much was left over.			

1	Surplusage. 10 cubits by 9,	For Back Wall of the	Surplusage 10 cubits by 9,	1
2	not required to cover	Holy of Holies, 10	not required to cover	2
3	any place.	cubits square.	any place.	3
	For length of	For length of	For length of	
4	South Wall of	Roof of	North Wall of	4
5	Holy of Holies, 10 cubits.	Holy of Holies, 10 cubits.	Holy of Holies, 10 cubits.	5
1	For length of	For length of	For length of	6
2	South Wall of	Roof of	North Wall of	7
3	Holy Place	Holy Place	Holy Place	8
4	20 cubits.	20 cubits.	20 cubits.	9
5	Depth of Wall 9 cubits.	Breadth of Roof 10 cubits.	Depth of Wall 9 cubits.	10

Left side labels: One Grand Curtain of Five. (rows 1–5); One Grand Curtain of Five. (rows 1–5)
Right side labels: One Grand Curtain of Five. (rows 1–5); One Grand Curtain of Five. (rows 6–9)

FROM MODEL TABERNACLE.
Scale—1/10 th of an inch to a cubit.
Waved line indicates where the two great curtains wer united by loops and taches.

As to surplusage, see appendix, chapter 27.

of five each were thus used, one for the holy place and the other for the holy of holies, is proved by Exodus 26:33, where it is said, "Thou shalt hand up the veil under the taches," that is before the entrance into the most holy place, and where the two grand curtains were united by the taches. Ten cubits of curtains spanning the roof (see diagram) show that the house was ten cubits broad. Thus the measurements of the curtains, like the length of the sockets (p. 6), and the breadth of the boards (p. 12), show that the tabernacle was thirty cubits (45 feet) long, and ten cubits (15 feet) broad.

5
THE GOAT-HAIR "TENT"
(EXOD. 26:14)

The goat-hair "tent" was a covering not "upon" or over the framework of golden boards, but "upon" or over the tabernacle (cherubim curtains; Exod. 26:1, with v. 7).

DIAGRAM OF ONE GOAT-HAIR CURTAIN, AND
ONE CHERUB CURTAIN.
FROM MODEL TABERNACLE.

GOAT-HAIR CURTAIN.

Part for South Wall 10 cubits.	Part for Roof 10 cubits.	Part for North Wall 10 cubits.

In all 30 cubits, and reaching to the ground on both sides (Exod. 26:8)

CHERUB CURTAIN.

1 cubit.	Part for South Wall 9 cubits.	Part for Roof 10 cubits.	Part for North Wall 9 cubits.	1 cubit.

In all 28 cubits (Exod. 26:2), and consequently one cubit at each side short of reaching the ground. Dotted lines indicate the ground.
Scale—¹⁄₁₀ th of an inch to a cubit.

Make curtains of goat hair for the tent over the tabernacle-eleven altogether (Exod. 26:7).

Every skilled woman spun with her hands and brought what she had spun-blue, purple or scarlet yarn or fine linen (Exod. 35:25).

There were eleven curtains made of goat-hair (Exod. 26:7), the usual material for tents in the East. Many of the goats of the East have black hair, but there are some species having fine white silky hair, like that of the Angora goat, and not a few writers are of opinion that it was hair of this goat or of one resembling it that was woven for the goat-hair curtains. Our model curtains are made of hair of the Angora goat. Women were the spinners (Exod. 35:25), and men the weavers (Exod. 36:8).

Size of the curtains.—Each curtain was 30 cubits long and 4 broad (see diagram above), that is two cubits longer than the finer curtains.

DIAGRAM OF THE TWO GREAT GOAT-HAIR CURTAINS;
ONE CONSISTING OF FIVE CURTAINS, AND THE OTHER OF SIX.
FROM MODEL TABERNACLE.

Fifty loops of blue.
Fifty loops of blue.

The sixth curtain of Exod. 26:9.

Scale—1/10 th of an inch to a cubit.

Disposition of the curtains.—As they were placed lengthways across the roof and down the side walls, they reached to the ground on both sides, as it was meet they should do, since they constituted the tent. But for their being two cubits longer than the cherubim curtains they would have been entirely concealed within the house, but these two additional cubits in their length allow of a cubit of the tent or goat-hair curtains being left uncovered within the house, and consequently exposed to view at the foot of the cherubim curtains; and if the material was of the fine

All the skilled men among the workmen made the tabernacle with ten curtains of finely twisted linen and blue, purple and scarlet yarn, with cherubim worked into them by a skilled craftsman (Exod. 36:8).

white, silky nature we have alluded to, it would appear as a beautiful white paneling on both sides of the sacred dwelling, and tend to set off to advantage the gorgeously adorned cherubim curtains, on roof and walls. These two cubits are evidently the two cubits alluded to in Exodus 26:13: "A cubit on the one side, and a cubit on the other side, of that which remaineth in the length of the curtains of the tent, it shall hang over the sides of the tabernacle (cherubim curtains, Exod. 26: 1, with v. 13), on this side and on that side to cover it," the space left uncovered by the cherubim curtains.

As for the additional length of the tent curtains, the half curtain that is left over is to hang down at the rear of the tabernacle (Exod. 26:12).

DIAGRAM OF THE ELEVEN GOAT-HAIR CURTAINS.

Illustrating the preceding remarks, and showing Five Curtains of the Grand Curtain of Six used for the roof and walls of the holy Place, and the half of another grand curtain used for the roof and side walls of the Holy of Holies, and the third of the other half hanging down back wall.

One Grand Curtain of Five.				Half of Grand Curtain.
1	Surplusage. Square	For Black Wall	Surplusage Square	1
2	of 10 cubits not required to	10 cubits square.	of 10 cubits not required to	2
	cover any place.		cover any place	
3	For	For	For	3
				Half of Grand Curtain.
4	length of South Wall of	length of Roof of	length of North Wall of	4
5	Holy of Holies 10 cubits	Holy of Holies 10 cubits.	Holy of Holies 10 cubits.	5
One Grand Curtain of Six.				One Grand Curtain of Six.
1	For length	For length	For length	6
2	of the	of Roof	of the	7
3	South Wall	of	North Wall	8
4	of Holy Place 20 cubits.	Holy Place 20 cubits.	of Holy Place 20 cubits.	9
5	Depth of Wall 10 cubits.	Breadth of Roof 10 cubits.	Depth of Wall 10 cubits.	10
6	4 cubits. The sixth curtain: "and shalt double the	sixth curtain in the fore-front	of the Tabernacle." 4 cubits.	11

Scale—1/10th of an inch to a cubit.

The eleventh curtain or the sixth of the grand curtain of six (diagram, p. 30), we are told, was doubled up in the forefront of the tabernacle, appearing as a beautiful triangular ornamental forefront. The five remaining ones of the grand curtain of six, spanned the roof and hung down the walls of the holy place, being the exact measure required. The half of the other grand curtain of five single curtains spanned the roof and hung down the south and north walls of the most holy place; and the remaining half of this great curtain 10 cubits long (the half curtain we suppose of Exodus 26:12), hung down the back wall 10 cubits deep, being the exact length required.

If the curtains being suspended within the house had a tendency to slightly incline the boards inward, this tendency could be counterbalanced by pins and cords on the outside of the edifice. Pins and cords are mentioned in connection with the tabernacle as well as with the court (Exod. 35:18).

All who are skilled among you are to come and make everything the LORD has commanded . . . the tent pegs for the tabernacle and for the courtyard, and their ropes (Exod. 35:10, 18).

6
THE TWO-FOLD SKIN ROOF
(EXOD. 26:14)

There were two sets of curtains within the house. Without there were two sets of skin coverings, forming the roof only, and not hanging down the walls as well, as many suppose. Should it be objected to this view that the golden boards would be exposed to the weather, the same objection might be urged with respect to the silver rods, silver capitals, and silver hooks of the court pillars, and also with respect to the five gold-covered pillars at the entrance of the tabernacle, which were all equally exposed to the effects of the weather. Further, on this point, see appendix, chapter 28.

The rams' skins, being tanned, were dyed red, and probably resembled the leather still sold in Syrian towns. The Israelites would find no difficulty in supplying them, since they were rich in flocks and herds.

Badgers' skins (seal or porpoise skins, RV).—It is generally agreed that "badger" is a wrong interpretation of the Hebrew word "tachash," but whatever animal is intended, whether it ranged the forest or swam the ocean, it must have had a tough hide, as leather made of it was used for the outermost covering of the tabernacle, being placed above that of the red rams' skins.

The Badger-Skin Covering

Ugly or beautiful?—It was likely of a sky-blue or other lovely color. Some tell us it was very ugly. The spiritually minded Soltau, in his *Tabernacle and the Priesthood,* says (p. 67), "The tabernacle must have appeared to the eye of a stranger as a long, dark, coffin-like structure." Several writers, charmed with Soltau's description, have been at pains to improve upon it, and in case we might not be sufficiently impressed with the ugliness, one of these writers asks us in imagination to ascend some commanding height, and get a good view of it. The Rev. George Rodgers, in his *Gospel according to Moses*, says (p. 34): "In this covering there was nothing beautiful or attractive. I can suppose a man to have looked down on the long, dark, coffin-like structure." The passage usually quoted to confirm this opinion is, "I have shod thee with badgers' skins," and hence the writers alluded to above imagine that the covering was ugly and shoe-black like. Such writers, however, appear to quote the text without even once looking it up in the Bible, a dangerous practice, for had they looked it up they would have seen that it was a very grandly dressed woman who was so shod, and with the design of making her not ugly but beautiful. From the crown of her head to the soles of her feet she was dressed in the most costly and splendid attire, and decked with the most precious and lovely ornaments. When so arrayed and shod with the badgers' shoes, it is said of her, "Thou wast exceeding beautiful" (Ezek. 16:9–15), and we have no doubt that the tabernacle, even with its badger-skin covering, like her and like the temple of which it was the prototype, was "exceeding beautiful."

The reason why Soltau and those who are influenced by his views are so anxious to see the tabernacle appear ugly is that it may typify Christ's humility and illustrate such passages as, "I am a worm and no man" (Ps. 22:6) and "When we shall see Him there is no beauty that we should desire Him" (Isa. 53:2). If such writers are correct, would analogy not lead us to expect that the high priest should have had sackcloth thrown over his golden garments, which we are told, were for glory and beauty?

He grew up before him like a tender shoot,
and like a root out of dry ground.
He had no beauty or majesty to attract us to him,
nothing in his appearance that we should desire him.
He was despised and rejected by men,
a man of sorrows, and familiar with suffering.
Like one from whom men hide their faces
he was despised, and we esteemed him not
(Isa. 53:2–3).

7
THE BEAUTIFUL DOORS

Hang the curtain from the clasps and place the ark of the Testimony behind the curtain. The curtain will separate the Holy Place from the Most Holy Place (Exod. 26:33).

There were two doors; an outer and an inner (Exod. 26:31–37). *The outer door* (or first veil, Heb. 9:2) was made of blue, purple, and scarlet, and fine twined linen yarn, and like the colored curtains, the work of the weaver, for although it is said in the *A.V.*, that the ornamental work was of needlework (v. 36), this term does not appear in the original. In the RV the Hebrew word is rendered "the work of the embroidered," and in the Variorum Bible, we have the work of the variegater; the original indicates work that might be executed either by needle or the loom.

For the entrance to the tent make a curtain of blue, purple and scarlet yarn and finely twisted linen—the work of an embroiderer (Exod. 26:36).

In the description of the cherubim curtains finest white linen yarn is first mentioned, and then the bright colors follow (Exod. 26:1) leading us to suppose that the ground-work or warp was of fine white linen. With respect, however, to the hangings for the doors, blue is first named (vv. 31–37), leading us to be of opinion that in their case the ground-work or warp was of blue yarn. And if blue, as likely, was the prominent color of the hangings, then this was significant, as these hangings were the doors of the dwelling, and more especially, as we shall see, with respect to the door of the holy of holies. With the

He carved cherubim, palm trees and open flowers on them and overlaid them with gold hammered evenly over the carvings (1 Kgs. 6:35).

purple, scarlet, and undyed white linen threads, beautiful devices were interwoven into the warp or ground work, probably consisting of palm trees and flowers such as adorned the corresponding door hanging of the temple, of which that of the tabernacle was the prototype (1 Kings 6:35).

The beautiful door hanging was suspended from the five golden pillars standing before the entrance of the tabernacle (v. 37).

The inner door (or second veil, Heb. 9:3), called the veil, was not only resplendent like the outer door hanging with blue, purple and scarlet and fine white linen, but besides was adorned all over with lovely cherubim figures, its chief characteristic. "With cherubim the work of the cunning workman shall it be made" (Exod. 26:31, RV).

This gorgeous curtain was suspended from the four golden pillars standing before the entrance into the holy of holies. It was called *the* veil (v. 31) whose chief prevailing color, most likely, as we have already remarked, was blue, and this is very significant, as it (*the* veil) was the type of the blue skies through which our Great High Priest passed into heaven, the true holy of holies (Luke 24:50–52; Acts 1:9–11).

Make gold hooks for this curtain and five posts of acacia wood overlaid with gold. And cast five bronze bases for them (Exod. 26:37).

Behind the second curtain was a room called the Most Holy Place (Heb. 9:3).

8

WITHIN THE CHERUBIM CURTAIN TABERNACLE

Make the tabernacle with ten curtains of finely twisted linen and blue, purple and scarlet yarn, with cherubim worked into them by a skilled craftsman (Exod. 26:1).

We have already tried to show the superiority of the splendid cherubim curtains, and would now still further try to emphasize their pre-eminence. They constituted the tabernacle (Heb. "dwelling"), and all the other parts of the sacred edifice are not mentioned till it has been described. They were made for it; and not it for them (Exod. 26:1–15). The golden boards, as already noticed, are not called the tabernacle but only the boards for the tabernacle (v. 1, with 15).

In imagination visit the sacred dwelling. Standing in the holy place and looking eastward, you observe that the door you entered by forms the east wall, whose loveliness at once attracts your attention. On a groundwork of blue, beautiful palm trees and flowers are interwoven with purple, scarlet and fine twined linen. As you turn round, the veil, forming the west wall of the apartment, now claims your notice. It is even more beautiful than the east wall, for it is not only radiant with the bright hues that adorned it, but in addition, shines all over with lovely cherubim figures. And now, as you turn your wondering and admiring eyes to the roof above you and then to the south and north walls, you see that like the veil they are all glittering with the shining cherubim, who seem to be regarding you with affection. On your right hand stands the golden table, on your left, the golden candlestick, and right before you at the far end of the chamber, the golden altar.

When now you enter the holy of holies your admiration increases. One wall, the east one of the holy place, is not enriched with cherubim, but all the walls, north, south, east and west, as well as the roof of this inner sanctuary in which you are now standing, are resplendent with the beautiful colors and with the bright shining cherubim. And besides these symbolic figures looking at you from roof and walls, there are two of solid gold on the mercy seat, on which by a visible symbol God was seated, and shone forth from between the cherubim. These beautiful and symbolic figures so crowd the holy of holies, that it may well be called the cherubim chamber.

The Levites, however, are to set up their tents around the tabernacle of the Testimony so that wrath will not fall on the Israelite community. The Levites are to be responsible for the care of the tabernacle of the Testimony (Num. 1:53).

Strange as it may seem, some writers confidently tell us that only one-third of these superb tapestry curtains, the part that formed the ceiling, was visible in the interior, and that the remaining two-thirds hung over the outside of the boards, and hid from view, being covered by the goat-hair tent. They are greatly mistaken, for curtains so rich and so beautifully adorned were certainly never intended otherwise than to be seen and to be wholly displayed in the interior, as we have shown they were. Those writers are not less in error who tell us that the greater part of the curtains covered the two internal sides of a sloping roof, and no part of the walls, and that the remainder extended outward from the sloping roof and formed dormitories for the priests (appendix, chapter 28). The entire curtains formed as was meet, and as their name indicates (Exod. 26:1), the dwelling of Israel's God and King. No part of them formed dwellings for the priests who had their tents with the rest of the Levites close to and around the tabernacle (Num. 1:53), and on what was considered holy ground.

Typical and Spiritual Significance of the Cherubim Curtain Tabernacle

It bears some analogy to the believer, to the church, to Christ, and to heaven.

First, To the believer. God who dwelt within the curtains, condescends to dwell graciously in the heart of every true Israelite; "Saints are an habitation of God through the Spirit" (Eph. 2:22). As the tabernacle was more beautiful within than without, so are God's children. They are clothed with the spotless robe of Immanuel's righteousness, and adorned with the graces of humility, love, holiness, and heavenly-mindedness. Arrayed in these, the King's daughter is all glorious within, and will shine forth with undiminished luster for ever and ever. These are the blue, and the purple, and the scarlet, that will never lose their bright and lively hues. Have you this spiritual embroidery, and is it shining out in your daily life? If so, happy are you. Strive by the aid of the Holy Spirit to shine more and more. No fast colors save these—all else will fade and die. Is it, however, otherwise with you? If so, come to Jesus. By faith ask Him to throw around you His own beautiful robe of righteousness, and He will do it. Ask Him to send the Holy Spirit, the Spiritual Embroiderer, to imprint on your souls His own lovely image, and to inwork in you the graces of faith, hope, love, and every other feature of His likeness, and He will send Him. And it will then be true of you, "Ye are a temple of God, and . . . the Spirit of God dwelleth in you (1 Cor. 3:16, RV).

Second, To the church. Believers, of whom the church is composed, although scattered among many sects of professing Christians, are yet all one in Christ Jesus. As the curtains, though woven separately, were afterward sewed together and formed two great curtains united into one tabernacle by loops of blue and clasps of gold, so God's children are knit together by the silver ties of affection, and bound together by the golden clasps of love. The union of saints on earth, though real and close, is not so apparent as it really is, in consequence of the imperfections of even the best of Christ's disciples, and of differences of opinion dividing them into various denominations, but even here they shall yet, "see eye to eye," and be seen to be one as they really are. For this the great Intercessor prayed while on earth, and for this He still prays, as He now stands in the true holy of holies:—"I pray that they all may be one, as Thou, Father, art in Me and I in Thee." God delights to dwell in the midst of the united company of believers, who are His household "and are built upon the foundation of the apostles and prophets, Jesus Christ Himself being the chief corner stone; in whom all the building fitly framed together groweth unto an holy temple in the Lord: In whom ye also are builded together for an habitation of God through the Spirit" (Eph. 2:20–22).

Third, To Christ. God dwells or tabernacles in the individual believer, and in the church composed of saints, but in Christ He dwells more gloriously than elsewhere. "In Him dwelleth all the fullness of the Godhead bodily." He is the "true tabernacle which the Lord pitched and not man,"—a shrine altogether lovely, and a pre-eminently meet habitation for the Deity. God dwelt within the curtains by a visible symbol, seen by no one, save the high priest, and by those who had spiritual discernment when Christ was sojourning in this world and saw God in Him: "He," said Christ, "that hath seen Me, hath seen the Father." Though He was in the form of man, His disciples beheld beams of the divine glory shining forth through His humanity (John 1:14). The saints in heaven also behold God in Him. There He is the "face of God," for as our faces are the medium of expression to our souls, so that of Jesus in heaven will be of God to us. When we look upon it with delight, we shall behold it radiant with the good pleasure of our heavenly Father. Christ in heaven is pre-eminently the tabernacle of God.

Fourth, To heaven. Who can doubt that the beautiful cherubim curtain tabernacle was a type of heaven? Heaven is the place of the most glorious manifestation of God's presence. There angels and saints behold God shining, not by a mere symbol as He did within the curtains, but in the face of Jesus Christ. There too are those glorious beings who are mighty in strength (and whose perfections and graces were shadowed forth in the cherubim that stood upon the mercy seat, and of those that adorned the roof and walls of the dwelling), even thousands and tens of thousands of holy angels, guardians of the saints while on earth, and their companions and fellow-worshippers for ever in the heavenly temple. What a glorious temple! Christ, the Shekinah, the face

Therefore, since we have a great high priest who has gone through the heavens, Jesus the Son of God, let us hold firmly to the faith we profess. For we do not have a high priest who is unable to sympathize with our weaknesses, but we have one who has been tempted in every way, just as we are — yet was without sin (Heb. 4:14–15).

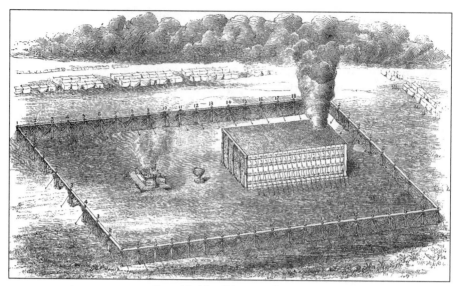

From Model.   Diagram of Court.

of God in the midst. Above, before, behind, on every side, all around myriads and myriads of bright angels and glorified saints, raising their celestial and unwearied voices in one glorious chorus, causing its exalted arches to ring with the praises of that Great High Priest who died for us, and now pleads our cause before the heavenly throne.

9
THE COURT OF GOD'S HOUSE

Having reared the beautiful tabernacle, we now go on to erect its surrounding lovely court, a double square, one hundred cubits long and fifty broad.

The boundary wall consisted of fine twined linen hangings, suspended from sixty pillars, spaced at the distance of five cubits from each other, twenty standing on the south, twenty on the north, ten on the west, and ten on the east, from whose four central pillars hung the bright attractive gate hanging, variegated with blue, purple, and scarlet yarn, the embroidery work probably consisting of trees, flowers, and other lovely devices (Exod. 27:9–19).

The Materials of the Pillars

We are not told of what material the pillars were. Although Exodus 27:10 seems to say the pillars were of brass, the original and the Revised Version do not indicate that they were, and the corresponding passage (Exod. 38:10) is silent on the subject, while in the account of the disposal of the brass offering (Exod. 38:29–31) the pillars are not mentioned as sharing in it.

From very careful calculations, we find that if the pillars had been of solid brass, they would have swallowed up the entire brass offering of 70 talents and 2400 shekels (Exod. 38:29), leaving none for the other uses to which it was to be put; while, on the other hand, if none of it had been used for the pillars, the quantity would have been much greater than was required. Hence, since there could have been neither

Make a courtyard for the tabernacle. The south side shall be a hundred cubits long and is to have curtains of finely twisted linen, with twenty posts and twenty bronze bases and with silver hooks and bands on the posts. The north side shall also be a hundred cubits long and is to have curtains, with twenty posts and twenty bronze bases and with silver hooks and bands on the posts (Exod. 27:9–11).

too much nor too little, it is evident that the pillars were constructed of wood and overlaid with brass; and this is in keeping with everything else, pertaining to the tabernacle and its court, made of wood, which without any exception was overlaid with metal, even with gold, silver, or brass.

The sockets, the basis of the pillars, were of brass. Their capitals were overlaid with silver, and also their fillets or rods extending from pillar to pillar all the way round. It is said in the text that the fillets were of silver, meaning in the sense of overlaying, as there was not enough of the solid metal to make them of. We read of the *brazen* altar, although it was only *overlaid with brass.* There were probably small apertures near the top of the pillars or through the capitals for the rods passing. Near the top of every pillar were two silver hooks, one on each side, to which the ends of two cords were attached, their other ends being attached to pegs which were fixed in the ground, and by this means the pillars were steadied and made to stand erect (Exod. 27:17–19).

The beauty of the wall.—The graceful pillars, like so many sentinels, encompassed and seemed to guard the sacred enclosure. Their silvery heads contrasted to advantage with their brazen feet and burnished bodies, and these, with the snowy whiteness of the hangings and the variegated gate, the tabernacle glittering with gold, and with its lovely sky-blue skin roof, tended still further to enhance the beauty of this superb wall of columns and fine twined linen.

The silver railing.—The silver capitals of the pillars, the silver connecting rods, and the silver hooks, formed one whole, a beautiful silver railing, from which was suspended the wall of white linen hangings, not unlikely, as some suppose, to have been on the reserved space outside of the sacred enclosure, beholding the services proceeding within.

The Origin of the Silver

Where did the silver laid out on this shining railing come from? The one hundred talents of ransom silver were entirely used up in forming the founda-

All the posts around the courtyard are to have silver bands and hooks, and bronze bases. The court-yard shall be a hundred cubits long and fifty cubits wide, with curtains of finely twisted linen five cubits high, and with bronze bases. All the other articles used in the service of the tabernacle, whatever their function, including all the tent pegs for it and those for the courtyard, are to be of bronze (Exod. 27:17–19).

tion of the tabernacle; but there was a fraction of
$^7/_{12}$ths of a talent (p. 9), equal to 1775 shekels more
than the hundred talents (Exod. 38:28). There is
never too much nor too little in the calculations of
the Divine Architect, as there is sometimes in those of
other architects, but always the exact quantity,
neither less nor more.

This fraction of silver was contemplated in the
divine plan. As directed (Exod. 38:28), it was used up
in the construction of the silver railing, on the top of
the pillars. The hundred talents formed a beautiful
silver lining below the sacred house, and upheld the
cherubim curtain tabernacle, with its goat-hair tent,
two-fold skin roof, and golden framework of boards;
and the one thousand, seven hundred and seventy-
five shekels were entirely used up on the railing which
upheld the court wall of linen hangings.

They used the 1,775 shekels to make the hooks for the posts, to overlay the tops of the posts, and to make their bands (Exod. 38:28).

The entire silver was thus devoted to the purpose
of upholding, and not a single grain of it was otherwise used. tabernacle and court alike were founded
on the price the Israelite men paid for their ransom.
Can anyone then reasonably doubt that the divine
architect was thereby foreshadowing the grand doc-
trines of redemption? If anyone doubt this let him try
to answer two questions—*First,* Why was no one
allowed to give silver save those who paid their
ransom with it? And, *Second,* Why was every grain of
silver thus paid devoted exclusively to the upholding
of the tabernacle and its court?

It is a most significant and suggestive fact that
Solomon's temple was founded on a rock. It is no
less a significant and suggestive fact that its great
prototype, the tabernacle, was founded on atonement
money.

The ransom silver lining shining below the
sacred dwelling was the beginning of the tabernacle,
and the ransom shining silver lining on the top of the
court pillars was the ending of the tabernacle—
redemption first and redemption last. And so of the
church. Christ our Redeemer is its beginning and
its ending, its first and its last, its alpha and omega,
its all in all.

When the pious Israelite looked down on the silver lining below the golden boards, and then up to the shining silver on the top of the court wall, he saw with a glad heart that tabernacle and court were borne up by the silver which he and the other Israelite men had given for their ransom. And when we who believe look down on what the church, of which we are members, is resting on, we see with a glad heart that it is the price of redemption, even of Him who gave Himself a ransom for sinners. "All other ground is sinking sand." And when we look up, as the Israelite did, to the atonement money shining of the top of the court pillars, our eyes are again fixed on our blessed Redeemer, and nothing in heaven and nothing in earth must come between us and Him to obscure our view. The brightest angel and the greatest saint must alike stand aside, that our eyes may see Jesus and Jesus only.

> My faith looks up to Thee,
> Thou Lamb of Calvary,
>   Savior Divine.

Purposes Served by the Court

The tabernacle court was the scene of worship, where the various offerings were received, and the sacrificial victims slain, and their blood poured out, and in which their carcasses, or parts of them, were consumed by fire. There is only one court spoken of in Exodus, though courts are frequently mentioned in the Psalms as pertaining to the tabernacle. The reference is sometimes to the temple, but not always. In Psalms written by David the tabernacle must be meant, as the temple was not erected till after his day. Some think that a line of demarcation divided the tabernacle court at the altar, and that none but priests and Levites were permitted to go beyond it, while Israelites bringing sacrifices and offerings might come thus far, but no farther. The court thus divided may have been regarded as two courts. May not the space between the Levitical tents and the tabernacle court have been regarded as a kind of outer court, where God's people might on occasions assemble, and through the meshes of the hangings be spectators of the sacred rites?

In the holy land the priests and Levites on duty at the tabernacle would still require to have their tents or houses around the outside of the court. The people, when bringing offerings, were allowed to enter the court, and approach at least as far as the altar; and doubtless, on other occasions as well, there was no bar to pious Israelites visiting the courts of the Lord's house. It is true the space within the linen walls could not accommodate many worshippers at a time, so that some arrangement would be necessary to prevent overcrowding; but if the space alluded to—the holy ground on the outside—was regarded as an outer court, a very large assembly might meet there. The Psalms prove that many of God's ancient people loved to visit the courts of the Lord's house, and were encouraged to wait upon Him there. "Enter into His gates with thanksgiving, and into His courts with praise" (Ps. 100:4). David's resolution was, "As for me, I will come into Thy house in the multitude of Thy mercy; and in Thy fear will I worship towards Thy holy temple" (tabernacle) (Ps. 5:7). Read also Psalm 27:4–6, where the reference is also the court or courts of the tabernacle, to worship in which David looked forward with holy resolution, ardent longings, and joyful anticipations. From experience he could predict of all who sincerely sought God in these courts: "They shall be abundantly satisfied with the fatness of Thy house" (Ps. 36:8). The pious Israelite's great desire to visit God's house is very strikingly and beautifully described in the eighty-fourth Psalm: "My soul longeth, yea, even fainteth for the courts of the Lord's house; my heart and my flesh crieth out for the living God." Read also Psalms 116 and 132.

One thing I ask of the LORD, this is what I seek: that I may dwell in the house of the LORD all the days of my life, to gaze upon the beauty of the LORD and to seek him in his temple (Ps. 27:4).

Lessons Suggested by the Court

We may learn from the preceding remarks— *First,* That there is an intimate connection between the improvement of the means of grace and eminent piety. David was pre-eminently holy. He was a man

How can I repay the L<small>ORD</small>
for all his goodness to me?
I will lift up the cup of
salvation
and call on the name of
the L<small>ORD</small>.
I will fulfill my vows to
the L<small>ORD</small>
in the presence of all his
people (Ps. 116:12–14).

"after the Lord's own heart." He never, however, would have attained this nobel distinction, had he not ardently thirsted for the courts of the Lord's house, and diligently improved the opportunities they afforded of worshipping God. Those who would advance in the divine life and like the psalmist, enjoy God's favor, will not attain their object unless they greatly love and diligently improve the services of the sanctuary.

Learn, *second,* That our connection with the Christian church lays us under obligations to improve the privileges it confers. The dispensation of religion in connection with the tabernacle was one of shadows and types—the one we live under, of truth and fulfillment. The high priest who officiated in the court of God's house was only the shadow of the great high priest who was to come, and all the bleeding victims slain at the altar, but the types of the one great sacrifice that was to be offered in the fullness of time. Yet pious Israelites so improved their religious privileges as thereby to become meet for the higher privileges of the upper sanctuary.

The privileges we enjoy are much greater than those enjoyed by God's ancient people, and consequently increase our responsibility: "Unto whom much is given, of them also much shall be required. It is our peculiar advantage to contemplate a Savior already come, One who has been crucified, buried, raised from the grave, and exalted to the right hand of the Majesty on high"—One who stands before the throne of God, and as the great high priest of His people, for ever pleads the efficacy of His own blood shed for sinners on Calvary. May we have an ever deepening sense of the greatness of our privileges, and be enabled so to improve them as to grow in grace, in the knowledge of our Lord and Savior Jesus Christ, and in meekness for the inheritance of the saints in light.

Learn, *third,* That those who delight in the services of the sanctuary will be admitted to heaven when they die.

Old Testament saints who loved to visit the courts of God's house are now worshipping in the temple not made with hands, and if we through eternity would like to tread the blessed uppercourts, we must, while in this world, in faith, and with holy relish, and ardent love, tread those of God's house on earth. If we are doing so, we have a bright prospect before us, for the same gates that opened to admit our great high priest into the new Jerusalem, will open for us too when the time of our departure comes, and we will go in, and from thenceforth serve God day and night in His holy temple for ever and ever.

10
THE BRAZEN ALTER

Make a horn at each of the four corners, so that the horns and the altar are of one piece, and overlay the altar with bronze (Exod. 27:2).

Having reconstructed the tabernacle and its court, we now proceed to supply them with beautiful and appropriate furniture, the various articles of which were called holy vessels. We begin with the first holy vessel reached on entering the court, and as its importance and the ends it served demanded, occupied a central and commanding situation, standing mid-way between the gate of the court and the door of the tabernacle. It was square in form, being 5 cubits long, 5 cubits broad, and 3 high (Exod. 27:1), made of acacia wood and overlaid on the outside with brass, as were also the projections called horns, one of which

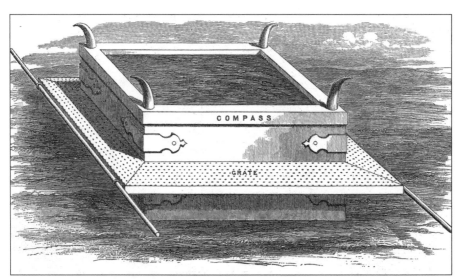

From Model.   The Brazen Altar.   Scale—1 inch to a cubit.

arose at each corner (v. 2). To these horns the animals to be sacrificed were sometimes bound. "Bind the sacrifice with cords, even unto the horns of the altar" (Ps. 118:27).

The compass (v. 5), probably, was a rim or border encircling the upper part of the altar (see view of altar, p. 48), probably less ornate than those of the ark, incense-altar, and shewbread table, and helping to compact its sides together. Without something of the kind, the court altar would have had a plainness and want of finish about it not in keeping with the rest of the sacred furniture.

The grate of network (vv. 4, 5), extending, in our opinion, like a shelf or ledge from the middle of the altar on the outside, served as a platform for the priests standing on when offering up sacrifices. Ashes falling accidentally off the altar would escape through the meshes of the grating, while fuel and pieces of the sacrifice would be caught. Though the altar itself had no rings, the grate had four, one at each of its corners (see view of altar, p. 48), and it was through these the staves passed by which the altar (not the grate merely) was carried (see Exod. 27:1–8; 38:1–7). This could not have been the case had the grate, as some suppose, formed the surface. Some think that the grate was suspended half-way down the inside of the altar, that the rings of the grate passed though holes in the altar to the outside, and that the rings so placed not only served as places of the staves passing through, but also to sustain the grate in its place. Anyone, however, may see that the fire so far down in the hollow of the altar was entirely unsuitable for the purpose required; and, further, that the fire would have burned the sides which within the altar were not overlaid with metal. The text merely says, referring to the outside, "thou shalt overlay it with brass" (Exod. 27:2), whereas when both outside and inside of any articles were to be covered with metal, the text distinctly says, "within and without shalt thou overlay it" (Exod. 25:11). Earth, therefore, of which the hollow of the altar must have been filled, would form the surface on which the fire burned (Exod. 20:24).

The poles are to be inserted into the rings so they will be on two sides of the altar when it is carried. Make the altar hollow, out of boards. It is to be made just as you were shown on the mountain (Exod. 27:7–8).

Fr. Von Meyer is substantially of our opinion. He considers, however, that the compass was the shelf or platform, and that the grate was its support, being placed under it and parallel with its outer edge. According to this plan the under half of the altar (including the compass and the grate) was broader

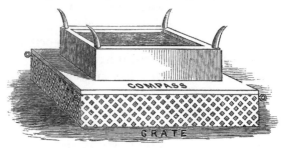

than the upper half. The above woodcut shows our model altar, with the compass and grate placed according to Meyer's opinion, and which the RV seems to favor. It renders the original not "compass" but "ledge."

The platform, whether the compass or the grating, being at the distance of only 1^1/$_2$ cubits (2^1/$_4$ feet) from the ground, a very gentle slope of earth could easily have led up to it at one or more sides.

Fire came out from the presence of the LORD and consumed the burnt offering and the fat portions on the altar. And when all the people saw it, they shouted for joy and fell facedown (Lev. 9:24).

Before leaving one place of encampment for another, the ashes and the fire were removed—the former cast away, and the latter probably placed in a fire-pan for the purpose of being transported. A cloth of purple was then spread over the top of the altar, and not unlikely fixed to the horns. On it the various vessels connected with the altar were placed, and then a cover of badger's skin spread over them. When all was ready for starting, the massive brazen framework was raised, and borne away by its bearers, the earth only being left behind.

The utensils of the altar were all made of brass (Exod. 27:3). Their varied uses are obvious—the "pan" for removing the ashes to a clean place (Lev. 4:12); "the shovel" for scraping the ashes together and placing them in the pan; the "basins" for holding the blood of the slain animals; "fleshhooks" for keeping the sacrifices in proper position on the fire, lifting up portions that might fall off, and retaining them on the altar; "fire-pans" for holding the fire when the surface of the altar was being cleared, and also for transporting it when the Israelites were on the march (Exod. 27:3).

The fire was kindled supernaturally (Lev. 9:24), and the divine command was, "The fire shall ever be burning, it shall never go out" (Lev. 6:13).

The Use of the Altar

The altar "Was to make reconciliation upon" (Lev. 8:15), between God and His sinful people. This was effected by the priests, who sprinkled upon it the blood of the atoning victims, and who also put their carcasses, or certain pieces of them, on the fire to be consumed. Hence, day by day, continually, new propitiatory animals were slain, fresh blood poured out, and the fire, ever crying "give, give," fed. The blood shed and poured out before and sprinkled upon the altar, was an atonement for the sins of the people. The death of the victim signified that the offerer deserved to die for his transgressions, and that its life was substituted for his. This was the appointed means of propitiating Jehovah—in other words, of procuring remission of sins, averting deserved wrath, such as the plague or other judgments, and securing to the people of Israel the continuance of the privileges and blessings which they enjoyed.

Moses slaughtered the bull and took some of the blood, and with his finger he put it on all the horns of the altar to purify the altar. He poured out the rest of the blood at the base of the altar. So he consecrated it to make atonement for it (Lev. 8:15).

These were merely temporal in their nature and participated in by all Israel. Pious Israelites, however, were more highly favored, for they were partakers not only of temporal, but also of spiritual and eternal blessings. And we believe that many, if not all, of those who were Israelites indeed, had glimpses more or less distinct, through the altar and the sacrifices, of the coming Messiah.

Typical and Spiritual Significance

Three words about the altar. *First,* It was a type of the cross—the wonderous cross on which the Prince of Glory died. He, the one great sacrifice for sin, was offered up on it. As reconciliation was made upon the altar, so the end of all sacrifices was attained by that which was presented on the cross: "And (having made peace through the blood of His cross) by Him to reconcile all things unto Himself, by Him,

I say, whether they be things in earth, or things in heaven. And you, that were sometime alienated and enemies in your mind by wicked works, yet now hath He reconciled" (Col. 1:20, 21). See, in the blood shed at and sprinkled upon the altar, the type of that blood which cleanseth from sin, and in the lamb slain and offered upon it every morning and evening, "the Lamb of God, slain from the foundation of the world." Yea! In every bleeding victim see the one great sacrifice, "Him who was once offered to bear the sins of many." And see in the priests who served at the altar Him who, in the fullness of time, offered Himself. Christ is both priest and sacrifice. No priest save Himself could have administered at the New Testament altar, and no victim but Himself could have bled and died on it for the sins of a world. The brazen altar, and the various sacrifices offered on it, had no meaning if they did not typify Christ. The blood of the sin-offerings was sprinkled on the altar's horns, which were symbols of power, protection, and salvation.

Second, The altar was sometimes used as a place of sanctuary where certain transgressors (such as those who had sinned ignorantly) were shielded by divine authority from punishment.

Others—for whom the law did not regard it as a refuge—sometimes fled to it in the vain hope of escaping the desert of their sins. Thither Adonijah fled from the wrath of Solomon, and laid hold on the horns of the altar, and continued clinging to them till he received the king's pardon (1 Kings 1:50–53). Thither also fled the wicked and treacherous Joab, and laid hold on the same horns, but they availed him not, for he was slain by the king's command even while clinging to them.

But Adonijah, in fear of Solomon, went and took hold of the horns of the altar (1 Kgs. 1:50).

We have an altar, even Jesus, who has never failed any poor sinners who have fled to Him, and by faith laid hold of His arms ever outstretched to save. No sooner are His arms grasped by faith than the penitent clinging one receives the king's pardon,— hears a voice coming down from the excellent glory, saying, "I, even I, am He that blotteth out thy transgressions."

Blessed Jesus, when to Thy cross we flee, and by faith lay hold on Thee, we are safe. The thunders of God's wrath may roll over our heads, and the lightnings of His vengeance flash all around us; our sins, like mountains may rise up before us, and the law may cry for vengeance; and devils and wicked men may unite for our destruction; yet none of these things can move us, harm us, or endanger our safety, while in our arms we hold Thee, blessed Jesus!

Third, The altar was a very conspicuous object in the court. It stood in the center, and when worshippers entered it was right before them. They could not fail to be impressed with its square and massive form, its bright and blood-stained exterior, its blazing fire, and the ascending curling smoke of the burning offerings, and its white-robed and ministering priests. If the type of the crucifixion was so very conspicuous in the court, how much more so should the crucified Christ Himself be in the New Testament church? As the devout Hebrew on entering the gate leading to the sacred precincts could not miss seeing the brazen altar, so believers when visiting the Christian sanctuary, should ever behold Jesus as its greatest attraction. The minister who does not make the cross the grand theme of his preaching, need not expect to lead sinners to the Savior.

As the altar was the most prominent of the holy vessels in the tabernacle court, and as its antitype, the cross of Christ, is the principal object held up in the pulpit by faithful ministers of the Gospel, so Christ is and ever will be the chief attraction of the New Jerusalem; and if we are among the number of the happy ones, to whom its golden gates will open when they die, we shall behold as we enter right before us Jesus all glorious in the midst, for the first scene that will burst upon our wondering and admiring gaze will be the "Lamb that once was slain;" and the first wave of celestial melody that will greet our ears and transport our hearts will be, not the song of angels— they cannot join in it—but the song of the redeemed, high above the song of angels, praising Him who loved us, and washed us from our sins in His own blood.

11
THE SHINING LAVER

This beautiful vessel, standing midway between the altar and the door of the tabernacle, was much more conspicuous and capacious than woodcut No. 1, and some writers would lead us to suppose.

This vessel consisted of two parts.

They made the bronze basin and its bronze stand from the mirrors of the women who served at the entrance to the Tent of Meeting (Exod. 38:8).

"The laver and his foot" (Exod. 38:8).—Both were likely roundish in form, the foot probably being flat, shaped somewhat like a saucer, and receiving its supply of water when needed from the laver which is supported aloft by a shaft or pillar arising from its center. The foot thus served as a basin, and the laver as a cistern large enough to contain at least a day's supply of water (see woodcut No. 2). The water would be drawn by cranes from the laver, as shown in the illustration. Cranes, though not shown in the illustration, would also be used for drawing off the water when it became impure from the foot or basin.

Made of brazen mirrors.—Ordinary brass seems not to have been sufficiently fine, pure, and transparent out of which to fashion this holy vessel. Nothing save brazen mirrors will suffice; and "the women assembling at the door of the tabernacle (tent of meeting)" parted with theirs for this sacred purpose (Exod. 38:8). Some writers tell us that Moses took the mirrors by force, but the text does not say so, neither should we. The laver, as it shines on the sacred page, is a striking and imperishable memorial of the zeal of God's house, and of the large-hearted liberality of the fair donors.

Washing at the laver.—Some writers say that the priests did not wash at the laver, but with water taken from it into other vessels; the text, however, seems rather to indicate that they washed at the laver itself: "Aaron and his sons shall wash their hands and feet thereat" (Exod. 30:19).

A basin and a mirror.—Made of the women's offering, the laver may have served the double purpose of a basin for the priests washing at, and a mirror for seeing themselves in, and this may have been the intention of its being made of the gifts of the generous givers. The priests were required to keep their persons and their garments spotlessly clean.

The use of the laver was mainly to hold water to
wash certain parts of the bodies of the animals slain as
sacrifices, and also and chiefly to wash the hands and
feet of the priests. The penalty for neglecting to wash
was very severe: "When they go into the tabernacle of
the congregation they shall wash with water that they
die not" (Exod. 30:20, 21).

Significance of the Washing with Water

The washing doubtless pointed to the unsullied
holiness of God, to the pollution of sin, and to the
purity of heart necessary in those who would render
acceptable worship. If the neglect of the mere outward
symbol of purity—the washing of the hands and feet
with water—was punishable with death, how hateful
must an impure heart be in the sight of Him who is of
purer eyes than to behold iniquity.

The priests were required to draw near to God,
not only with clean hands and feet, but with a pure
heart. No worship rendered by anyone can be pleasing to God, the Holy One of Israel, however clean the
hands, if the heart be polluted.

What the Washing with Water Symbolized

Washing with water is frequently mentioned in
the New Testament (Eph. 5:26; John 3:3–5; Heb. 10:22),
and in every instance it is unmistakably evident that
the cleansing of the soul from the defilement of sin is
to be understood. How shall we become the subjects
of inward purification? Believers are sanctified
through the Word (John 15:3; 17:17): Christ's prayer
to His Father for His people is "Sanctify them
through Thy truth. Thy word is truth." "Christ died,"
we are told, "that He might redeem us from all iniquity and purify unto Himself a peculiar people," and
the saints in heaven are said to have washed their
robes and made them white in the blood of the Lamb.
We must, however, never forget that it is the Holy
Spirit that takes of the things of Christ and shows
them to us; that it is He who makes the truth effectual
both for the conversation of sinners and the sanctifi-
cation of believers, and that it is He who is peculiarly
associated in the Scriptures with the cleansing of the

soul (1 Cor. 6:11; Titus 3:5). The brazen altar typically pointed to the atoning work of Christ, and the laver to the sanctifying work of the Holy Spirit. If the brazen altar shows us that the guilt of sin can be canceled by the blood of Christ alone, the laver no less significantly teaches that the defilement of sin can be washed away by no other agency than that of the Holy Spirit.

> 'Tis Thine to cleanse the heart,
>   To sanctify the soul,
> To pour fresh life on every part
>   And new-create the whole.

Jesus answered, "I tell you the truth, no one can enter the kingdom of God unless he is born of water and the Spirit" (John 3:5).

The Altar and the Laver

The only articles of furniture in the Court were inseparable companions. Neither of them could be dispensed with if the ministering priests were to discharge the various services of the tabernacle. The New Testament altar and laver are also inseparably connected in the Christian dispensation. In order to be saved we need not only to be cleansed from the guilt, but also from the pollution, of sin—not only to receive forgiveness of sins, but also to be cleansed inwardly "by the washing of regeneration and renewing of the Holy Ghost." Let us ever remember that in the salvation of the soul these two—the altar and the laver—can never be parted, for there can be no deliverance from the guilt of sin, apart from purity of heart and holiness of life. The voice we hear from the altar is, "Without shedding of blood is no remission." Let us also bend our ears and give heed to the voice that comes no less authoritatively from the laver saying, "Without holiness no man shall see the Lord," enjoy the light of his countenance now, and be admitted when he dies into heaven, the dwelling-place of God.

. . . he saved us, not because of righteous things we had done, but because of his mercy. He saved us through the washing of rebirth and renewal by the Holy Spirit (Titus 3:5).

The priests, without washing dared not, on penalty of death, enter the house made with hands, and none but those who have been cleansed by the washing (laver) of regeneration, and renewing of the Holy Spirit, will ever enter the one "not made with hands," where all the ransomed are kings and priests unto God for ever and ever.

12

THE SHEWBREAD TABLE

Leaving the court and its brazen altar and shining laver behind, we now, by the beautifully colored embroidered door, enter the first apartment of the sanctuary, called the holy place, to inspect its golden vessels. This, as we have already seen, was a very splendid chamber, twenty cubits long by ten broad. The ceiling above, the walls on both sides, and the veil before us, are all aglow with blue, purple, scarlet, and lovely bright cherubim.

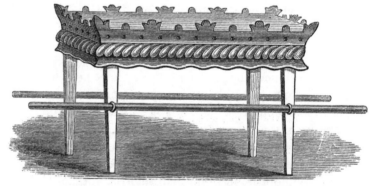

From Model.   Table of Shewbread.   Scale—1 inch to a cubit.

Moses placed the table in the Tent of Meeting on the north side of the tabernacle outside the curtain and set out the bread on it before the LORD, as the LORD commanded him (Exod. 40:22–23).

The table of shewbread, standing on the right hand or north side (Exod. 40:22), made of acacia wood and overlayed with gold (v. 23), measured 2 cubits long, 1 broad, and 1^1/$_2$ high (Exod. 25:23). The top of the leaf was encircled by an upright ornamental rim or crown of gold (v. 24), probably serving to prevent articles from falling off the table. The legs were united and the framework compacted by a handbreadth border

(3 inches) with a golden crown round about (v. 25). The four rings through which the gold-covered staves passed for carrying the table were placed at the four corners over against the border (vv. 27, 28).

Utensils in connection with the table.—There were several utensils in connection with the table (Exod. 25:29), all made of gold, but the purposes they served are not mentioned. The dishes are supposed to have been plates for the shewbread being placed on; the bowls, for holding the wine, poured out as libations in the holy place; the spoons or cups, for holding the frankincense, set on each pile of bread.

The bread was made of fine unleavened flour (Lev. 24:5–9). Twelve cakes in two piles of six each, always stood on the table, called on that account the perpetual or continual bread (Num. 4:7). It was also named the bread arranged in order, the reason for which is obvious (Exod. 40:23). The more significant name we shall notice presently. On the top of each pile was placed

Take fine flour and bake twelve loaves of bread, using two-tenths of an ephah for each loaf. Set them in two rows, six in each row, on the table of pure gold before the LORD (Lev. 24:5–6).

Frankincense, probably in the cups we have spoken of. It is thought by some that the frankincense was burned once a week when the bread was being renewed; and by others that it was ever burning, which does not appear very likely, as the quantity consumed would be very great. There may, however, have been some means whereby it could be slowly consumed, and kept always burning: in that case the holy place would be ever fragrant.

Presence bread.—The bread was called the "shewbread" (Heb. "bread of faces" or presence bread), because it was in God's dwelling-place, and before the symbol of His presence, the veil only intervening.

The renewal of the bread.—The bread was renewed every Sabbath by fresh loaves. The loaves removed belonged to the priests, and could be eaten by them only, and in the holy place and nowhere else. All thank-offerings were holy, and this one peculiarly so: "It is most holy unto Him of the offerings made by fire" (Lev. 26:9).

Offerings Presented in the Holy Place

Only the shewbread, the incense offerings, and the wine for a libation or drink-offering were presented in the holy place. Although it is not expressly said that wine stood on the table, it is evident the bowls (Exod. 25:29) were intended for holding and pouring out wine. To "cover withal" (v. 29) means in the original "to pour out withal;" and is so rendered in the Revised Version. All the other offerings were brought to the brazen altar in the court. The ceremonies connected with all the sacrifices were soon over, except in the case of the shewbread: "He" (that is, Aaron and his successors) "shall set it in order before the Lord continually" (Lev. 24:8). It is said to be made by fire, as the frankincense burning on the bread (Lev. 24:7) constituted one and the same offering.

Along each row put some pure incense as a memorial portion to represent the bread and to be an offering made to the LORD by fire (Lev. 24:7).

Significance of the Shewbread

As far as the shewbread is considered merely in the light of a peace or thank-offering, there is no difficulty concerning it. Probably as the tabernacle was the residence of Israel's Divine King, the idea of a palace was thereby, along with the other arrangements, carried out. Thus, the ark or throne, the golden candlestick, the incense-altar, the shewbread table, with its bread and wine, may have been regarded as the requisite furniture and provisions, and the priests as the servants who waited upon the King, and mediated between Him and the people. The Israelites, represented by the twelve loaves, acknowledged their dependence on God as the giver of the staff of life, and evinced their gratitude in giving Him part of what they owed solely to His bounty. The shewbread, ever lying on the table, was thus a constant memorial of God's goodness in providing for the nourishment of His people.

Our Indebtedness to God

We are as much indebted to the Great Giver for the staff of life, and for all other temporal blessings, as the Israelites were; and it is our duty, as much as it was theirs, to testify our gratitude by offering Him part of what He has given us; not that He stands personally in need of our gifts any more than He stood in need of the shewbread, but that His poor saints, and His cause or church in the world, may be benefited thereby; and that our own gratitude and sense of dependence on Him for all temporal, as well as spiritual, blessings, may be kept ever alive within us. "To do good and to communicate forget not: for with such sacrifices God is well pleased."

I am the living bread that came down from heaven. If anyone eats of this bread, he will live forever. This bread is my flesh, which I will give for the life of the world (John 6:51).

Christ the Bread of Life

Some are of opinion that the shewbread was a figure of Christ. Whether this be so or not, it is true that bread is a striking emblem of Him, and He Himself says, "I am the bread of life." May we feed by faith on Him, and our souls will be nourished unto eternal life. May our prayer be, "Lord, evermore give us this bread."

Blessings Partaken of in the New Testament Church

Some regard the bread and wine as representing the spiritual nourishment which may be had in the New Testament church. It is true, only the priests were permitted to eat the shewbread; but genuine believers are a royal priesthood, and they are all invited to sit at the New Testament table, and partake of its manifold blessings. "Eat ye that which is good, and let your soul delight itself in fatness."

The Good Things in the Heavenly Temple

May not the golden table point to the abundant supply of good things prepared in the heavenly temple for all those whom Christ will make kings and priests unto God for ever? There, a table is spread before His face, that is continually furnished with new wine and heavenly manna, with which the ransomed of the Lord will be refreshed and made glad. "In Thy presence is fullness of joy; at Thy right hand there are pleasures for evermore."

13
THE GOLDEN ALTAR

Make two gold rings for the altar below the molding—two on opposite sides—to hold the poles used to carry it (Exod. 30:4).

In the center, at the west end of the holy place, and just before the door-hanging of the holy of holies, stood the altar of incense, a situation of higher honor than that of any other of the sacred vessels we have yet considered, being regarded as immediately before the throne itself, even though the veil intervened. "Thou shalt put it before the veil, that is by the ark of the testimony, where I will meet with thee" (Exod. 30:6).

Like other altars, it was four-square, measuring 1 cubit long, 1 broad, and 2 high; its length and its breadth being thus equal. It was made of acacia wood, and overlaid with gold: "and thou shalt overlay it with pure gold, the top (Heb. "roof") thereof, and the sides (Heb. "walls") thereof round about, and the horns thereof" (v. 3).

Around the top was an ornamental crown or rim of gold; beneath, perhaps a little higher up than in our woodcut, and at two of the corners, according to the Authorized Version, were two gold rings for the gold-covered staves passing through, by which it was carried. The rings and staves so put seem to indicate that this holy vessel was carried corner-wise, and was so placed in the holy place, presenting to one entering a corner and not a side. The object of this arrangement, it is thought, was that a horn of the altar might point to each of the four great armies of Israel encamped around the tabernacle. The Hebrew word, however, rendered "corners" in the text (v. 4) is "ribs," so that the rings may not have been at the corners, but at the sides, one being in the center at the one side, and the other in the center, at the opposite side, and if so, the altar would not, as above, have been carried or placed corner-wise.

From Model. The Golden Altar. Scale—1 inch to a cubit.

The Purpose the Golden Altar Served

At first Aaron offered incense upon the golden altar, and afterward, on great occasions, the high priest did so; but ordinarily the duty was discharged by a priest, chosen weekly by lot, every morning and evening (Luke 1:9–11).

Incense was made of various sweet-smelling and precious spices, according to divine directions (Exod. 30:34). A similar compound, for any other purpose, was not allowed to be made, and no other than this could be used as incense. When the incense was to be offered, a fire pan or censer, with live coals from the brazen altar, was put upon the golden altar for burning it. The clouds of smoke arising from it were full of perfume, and spread their fragrance all around, penetrating the veil, and reaching even to the throne.

Then the LORD said to Moses, "Take fragrant spices—gum resin, onycha and galbanum—and pure frankincense, all in equal amounts" (Exod. 30:34).

The priest, while presenting this offering, was the people's intercessor with God, praying for them, and asking Him to hear and answer their petitions. Not that incense had any propitiatory significance—the animal sacrifices alone had that, without propitiation there is no access to God—but then the horns of the altar were sprinkled with atoning blood (Exod. 30:10; Lev. 16:18), so that it was from a blood-sprinkled altar that the sacred odors arose, bearing on their wings Israel's cry for mercy and all-needed blessings.

Then he shall come out to the altar that is before the LORD *and make atonement for it. He shall take some of the bull's blood and some of the goat's blood and put it on all the horns of the altar (Lev. 16:18).*

Typical and Spiritual Significance

The burning of incense in the holy place is regarded as an emblem of prayer. David so employed it: "Let my prayer be set before Thee as incense, and the lifting up of my hands as the evening sacrifice" (Ps. 141:2). And John, in his vision of heaven, tells us that when he had taken the book, "the four beasts (living creatures) and four-and-twenty elders fell down before the Lamb, having every one of them harps, and golden vials full of odors (incense), which are the prayers of saints" (Rev. 5:8). As the sweet fragrance of smoking incense is most agreeable to the senses, so are the prayers of God's children very pleasing and acceptable to Him.

The brazen altar is considered a type of Christ with respect to His atonement, and the golden altar a type of Him with respect to the other part of His priestly office—His intercession. Christ not only bled for us on the cross, a sacrifice for our sins, He also pleads for us before the heavenly throne. He is our advocate with the Father. The golden altar was before the ark or throne, the veil, however, being suspended between; but Christ—and with no intervening veil—is before the throne in heaven. It was from an altar with blood-sprinkled horns that the evening and morning incense ascended, and so when our great high priest intercedes for us on high, it is on the ground of His atoning sacrifice. See in His pierced hands and feet the blood-sprinkled horns. The very hands He holds up are those that were once nailed to the accursed tree.

From before the heavenly throne He is now looking down lovingly upon all His believing people, inviting and encouraging them to offer up their prayers, and assuring them that He Himself will present them, and secure gracious answers in the bestowal of rich and soul-satisfying blessings. Are you one of His believing people? If so, bend your ear and listen to His encouraging voice as it comes rolling down from the golden altar: "Hitherto have ye asked nothing in My name: ask and ye shall receive, that your joy may be full."

> Thou standest at the altar,
>   Thou offerest every prayer;
> In faith's unclouded vision
>   We see Thee ever there.
>
> Out of Thy hand the incense
>   Ascends before the throne,
> Where Thou art interceding,
>   Lord Jesus, for Thine own.—Eddis.

From Model.   The Golden Candlestick.

14

THE SEVEN BRANCHED GOLDEN CANDLESTICK

This splendid lamp-bearer standing on the left hand, or south side of the holy place (Exod. 40:24), was made entirely of pure gold, and of beaten work, that is it was not cast in a mold, but formed by the hand (Exod. 25:31). It and its utensils were made of a talent of pure gold (v. 39) equal to 1500 ounces, worth about £60000 at the present day, and probably of greater value in the days of Moses.

Make a lampstand of pure gold and hammer it out, base and shaft; its flower-like cups, buds and blossoms shall be of one piece with it (Exod. 25:31).

A talent of gold, however, forms but a very small block, and the probability is that the lamp-bearer was hollow; and about 2^1/$_3$ cubits (3 feet 6 inches) high. It could hardly have been higher, for the golden altar was 2 cubits (3 feet) high, and the lamps would require to burn at an elevation a little higher than this in order to afford sufficient light to the priests who ministered at the altar.

The candlestick got by Titus from the temple, if not that of the tabernacle, was evidently one after the same Divine pattern and of the same size. By comparing the representation of it (p. 68) taken from the Triumphal Arch with its bearers, averaging their height at 5 feet 10 inches, we find the candlestick to have been 3 feet high. But by comparing the candlestick with its bearers in a photograph we got recently from Rome for the purpose (see p. 69) we find the candlestick according to it, to be 2^1/$_3$ cubits (3 feet 6 inches) high which agrees with the height we suppose it to have been.

The circumstance that heathen devices appear on the base of the candlestick, has led some to assert

Bas-Relief from the Arch of Titus, showing the Golden Candlestick, and Table of Shewbread.

that the Romans provided the base. This, however, is by no means certain, for the original must have had a base, and on it the devices may have been wrought. See "The Peregrinations of the Golden Candlestick," appendix, chapter 30.

Members of the Golden Candlestick

From the under part or base the chief or upright branch, sprang not "branches" as in Exod. 25:31, but "branch" as correctly rendered in the corresponding passage (Exod. 37:17). See also Revised Version. The base and this upright branch or stem constituted the candlestick proper (Exod. 25:31–38), out of which came six branches like arms, three out of the one side, and three out of the other (v. 32). Both threes were parallel to each other, and they all curved upwards to an equal level. The main or upright branch probably rose to a height a little higher than the others.

Six branches are to extend from the sides of the lamp-stand—three on one side and three on the other (Exod. 25:32).

The Ornamentation

consisted of bowls, knops and flowers. The bowls were almond shaped (Exod. 25:33), of which there were three (v. 33) on each of the arms, and four (v. 34) on the shaft. The knops, it is supposed, were roundish in shape, like an orange or pomegranate. The knops probably occupied the corresponding position in the candlestick that capitals do in pillars,

From a photograph of the Arch of Titus, referred to at p. 68

and as there was only one knop to a branch, it would constitute the head of the branch, and so shaped as to suit it to hold, or fix a lamp to. There were, however, four (v. 34) knops mentioned in connection with the shaft, three of which occupy positions different from what could be found on the branches, showing that there was only one knop to each of the six branches. The position on the shaft for three of its four knops, is below the places where each pair of branches emerge, and the purpose the knops there seem to serve is to bear them up. The first or undermost knop would thus be the capital of the first division of the shaft or pillar bearing up the first or undermost pair of branches; the second knop would be the capital of the second division bearing up the second pair of branches; the third knop would be the capital of the third division bearing up the third pair of branches; and the fourth knop would be the capital at the top of the shaft, and like those at the end of each branch, so formed, as already mentioned, to suit it to hold a lamp—the shaft or stem being thus a kind of compound pillar (p. 66).

And on the lampstand were four cups shaped like almond flowers with buds and blossoms (Exod. 37:20).

Some, however, mention that each of the six branches had three knops, and in favor of this view, quote Exod. 25:34: "And in the candlestick (shaft) shall be four bowls, made like unto almonds with their knops and their flowers." From this text they seek to show that though one knop only is mentioned in connection with the branches, it is to be understood that all the bowls had knops and flowers. But the two "theirs" should be "its"—the pronoun being singular in the Hebrew. In the corresponding text (Exod. 37:20) the pronoun, as it ought to be, is in the singular, so that "its knops and its flowers" refer to the shaft or central branch, and not to the bowls; and consequently the above passages, while they show that the shaft had more knops than one, by no means prove that the six branches had more than one each.

We cannot gather from the text what the bowls, knops, and flowers, were intended to represent. They may, as some think, have consisted of buds, blossoms, and fruit, but whatever they may have stood for, they were exquisitely graceful and lovely figures, and were with the rest of the magnificent lamp-bearer skillfully formed by the hands of inspired artificers with the finest and most delicate tools imaginable. It is specially mentioned that the candlestick was fashioned "according unto the pattern the Lord had showed to Moses" (Num. 8:4).

The Gem of the Golden Vessels

For gracefulness of form, and the loveliness and elaborateness of its chaste and refined ornamentation, it surpassed all the other vessels of the Sanctuary.

The surpassing beauty and resplendent brightness of the golden candlestick, shining clear as a mirror with its seven soft clear brilliant lights, rendered it a most striking and imposing object.

The Oil

Supplying the lamps was pure olive oil, obtained from olives, not ground in a mill, but beaten (Exod. 27:20) in a mortar, to render the oil finer than by grinding.

Command the Israelites to bring you clear oil of pressed olives for the light so that the lamps may be kept burning (Exod. 27:20).

The Lamps Burned Always

It is difficult to understand from the various passages bearing on the subject, whether the lamps burned both day and night, or only during the night—some passages apparently favoring the one view, and some the other. Thus, "To cause the lamp to burn always" (Exod. 27:20); and "Command the children of Israel, that they bring unto thee pure olive oil, beaten for the light, to cause the lamp to burn continually" (Lev. 24:2).

These passages seem to teach that the lamps burned both day and night. If they do not teach that, the meaning must be, that "continual" and "always" signify at regular intervals, as in the case of some ordinances and offerings which are called perpetual, though occurring only at intervals. The other view, that they burned only during the night, seems to be supported by "Aaron and his sons shall order it from evening to morning" (Exod. 27:21): "And Aaron shall burn thereon (the golden altar) sweet incense every morning, when he dresseth the lamps" (Exod. 30:7, 8). From these texts it would appear that the lamps burned only during the night. If they were not intended to teach that, the meaning must be that the lamps were dressed in the morning, probably, one after another, not necessitating more than one being extinguished at a time, and after being lighted, burned during the day, the lamps receiving such further attention in the evening as admitted of their burning till the morning. As there were no windows in the tabernacle, and the priests had duties to

Aaron must burn fragrant incense on the altar every morning when he tends the lamps. He must burn incense again when he lights the lamps at twilight so incense will burn regularly before the LORD for the generations to come (Exod. 30:7–8).

perform during the day in the holy place, it is almost certain the lamps burned both night and day.

The Significance of the Candlestick and its Lamps

With oil, a symbol of the Holy Spirit, priests and kings were anointed, but all true believers have the Holy Spirit Himself poured out upon them. Their bodies are His temple: He is within every believer, as the candlestick was within the sanctuary, a source of light and life and comfort. He is also in the church; all its true light is from Him, and the light emanating from Him, as the number seven indicates, is sufficient, perfect, complete; nothing more is needed in order to ensure the purity, righteousness, and glory of the church. The very number is expressly applied to the Spirit, and one cannot help thinking that the reference is to the seven lamps of the golden candlestick: "Grace be unto you, and peace, from Him which is, and which was, and which is to come; and from the seven Spirits which are before the throne" (Rev. 1:4).

As the first apartment in the tabernacle was illuminated by the sevenfold light of the candlestick, and as the church composed of all genuine believers on earth in every age, is enlightened by the Holy Spirit, so will the church triumphant in heaven, that great temple, not made with hands, be a place of glorious light; and the light will never go out, it will burn always; so that there will be no night there; nor sun, nor moon, nor stars will shine in that happy place— "For the glory of God did lighten it, and the lamp thereof is the Lamb" (Rev. 21:23, RV).

Titus evidently thought that he had secured a rich and rare prize in the golden candlestick, seeing he caused it to be highly and conspicuously exalted in the triumphal procession to Rome (woodcut, p. 68). See "The Peregrinations of the Golden Candlestick," appendix, chapter 30.

15
THE ARK OF THE COVENANT

Leaving the first apartment of the tabernacle, and its lovely and richly ornamented vessels, the table of shewbread, the seven branched candlestick and altar of incense behind, we now pass beyond the veil, and enter the most holy place, the throne room of Israel's God and King. Let us approach with deepest reverence, put off our shoes, for if any place surely this we now tread is holy ground. Like the New Jerusalem of which it was the type, it was four square, "the length and the breadth and the height of it are equal" (Rev. 21:16), being 10 cubits long, 10 broad, and 10 high. Each of its sides—roof, floor, and north, south, east and west walls—was square, being 10 cubits by 10. It outshone in splendor the holy place, one of whose walls, the east one, forming the door, had no cherubim displayed on it; but, as we have already seen, every one of the four walls and roof of the most holy place, was resplendent with blue, purple, scarlet and bright shining cherubim, and besides those glowing on roof and walls, two of solid gold stood on the mercy seat. In this innermost chamber of the Great King stood the

The city was laid out like a square, as long as it was wide. He measured the city with the rod and found it to be 12,000 stadia in length, and as wide and high as it is long (Rev. 21:16).

Ark of the Covenant,

the chief and most sacred of all the objects connected with the dwelling, and for which the tabernacle itself, and all its brazen and golden furniture were made subordinate, and to which all the ministrations and ritual associated with them had reference. Its preeminence is further indicated in its being the first

From Model. The Ark of the Covenant. Scale—1 inch to a cubit.

thing connected with the tabernacle God spoke to Moses about, and commanded to be made (Exod. 25:10–22), and besides, in its being used in the temple (1 Kings 8:6), whereas all the other articles of furniture were superseded by new ones.

It consisted of four distinct objects:—1*st*, the ark proper; 2*nd*, the mercy seat; 3*rd*, the cherubim; and 4*th*, the shekinah.

The priests then brought the ark of the LORD's *covenant to its place in the inner sanctuary of the temple, the Most Holy Place, and put it beneath the wings of the cherubim (1 Kgs. 8:6).*

The Ark,

a box or chest made of acacia wood, and overlaid both within and without with pure gold, was $2^1/_2$ cubits long and $1^1/_2$ high and broad (Exod. 25:10–22).

It was surrounded at or over the top by an ornamental rim or crown of gold (v. 11). The rings for the staves passing through, are said in the Authorized Version to have been placed in the four corners. This, however, is a mistranslation, for the Hebrew word, rendered corners, is "feet"; so that the sacred chest had four feet, and on them the rings were fixed—not at the front and back as they are sometimes represented, but at the ends or short sides, so that the gold-covered staves or poles always remained in their places, as well when the ark was at rest in the sanctuary, as when being carried from place to place (Exod. 25:15), and could be drawn out as stated in 1 Kings 8:8. The rings and poles so placed would cause the ark to be more elevated when being transported than the rest of the sacred furniture, this being necessary, as it was a kind of leading standard and borne by priests or Levites (Num. 4:15; 3:31; Josh. 3:3; Deut. 31:9, 25) in the forefront (Num. 10:33) of the army.

The poles are to remain in the rings of this ark; they are not to be removed (Exod. 25:15).

Things Put into the Ark

In this sacred chest were deposited—

1. The tables of stone on which the ten commandments were written with the finger of God: "Put into the ark the testimony which I shall give thee." In these commandments God testified or showed His will, and they were evidence that He had made a covenant with the Israelites. If obedient they would be a testimony in their favor; if disobedient they

would, like the rest of the Scriptures afterward given them and placed in the same repository, testify against them (Deut. 31:26). Hence the sacred chest is sometimes named the ark of testimony. It is also called the ark of the covenant, as the moral law formed the basis of the covenant, or gracious agreement, God made with the Israelites, and in which he promised to be their God, and to regard them with favor on condition of their obedience.

2. A golden pot containing manna was laid up before the testimony. Moses by divine directions instructed Aaron to do this (Exod. 16:33, 34); and,

3. Aaron's budding rod was likewise laid before the testimony (Num. 17:10). Some are of the opinion that the pot and rod were not put in the ark, but merely placed beside it. This view is seemingly supported by 1 Kings 8:9, which states that it contained only the two tables of stone. The probability is that the pot and rod were lost during the time when the sacred chest was in the possession of the Philistines, for it's expressly stated in Hebrews 9:4 that they were once in it.

A casket has never before nor since contained such precious relics as these.

The Mercy Seat or Propitiatory

(see Hilasterion, Rom. 3:25) was made of solid gold, and was of the same length and breadth as the sacred chest itself (Exod. 25:17), and probably kept in its place by the ornamental crown encircling the ark (v. 11).

Typical and Spiritual Significance

Though the mercy seat or lid in the original is simply a cover (Kapporeth), it is spoken of in the text as distinct from the ark, and doubtless had a deeper meaning than its mere literal one, and signified to cover sin in the sense of forgiving sin. It was the place where God showed Himself merciful in forgiving sin, and hence it was called the mercy seat; it was, however, in consequence of the blood sprinkled on the mercy seat, that God was propitiated, and forgave the sins of

So Moses said to Aaron, "Take a jar and put an omer of manna in it. Then place it before the LORD to be kept for the generations to come." As the LORD commanded Moses, Aaron put the manna in front of the Testimony, that it might be kept (Exod. 16:33–34).

. . . This ark contained the gold jar of manna, Aaron's staff that had budded, and the stone tablets of the covenant (Heb. 9:4).

Make an atonement cover of pure gold—two and a half cubits long and a cubit and a half wide (Exod. 25:17).

the people. The blood sprinkled was typical of Christ's shed blood, through or by means of which God dispenses pardon and all the blessings of salvation to those who believe in Jesus. How appropriately then is Christ called the "Propitiatory" (Romans 3:25). God is now seated on a throne of mercy—of mercy because sprinkled with the blood of the Lamb; and transgressors, though their sins be as scarlet, may, without the intervention of priest or minister, approach—nay, are invited and entreated to come.

God presented him as a sacrifice of atonement, through faith in his blood. He did this to demonstrate his justice, because in his forbearance he had left the sins committed beforehand unpunished— (Rom. 3:25).

In letters of blood, His own precious blood, our Great High Priest has written on the mercy seat in heaven, the crowning gospel invitation, "Him that cometh unto Me I will in no wise cast out."

The Cherubim

were two gold figures, made of the same piece of gold as the mercy seat (Exod. 25:18) on which they stood, "one cherub on the one end and one cherub at the other end" (v. 19). It is generally supposed that they were in the form of male or female human figures.

They had wings stretching upwards and meeting on high (v. 20), forming a kind of canopy, and faces looking to each other (v. 20) with a downward bend to the mercy seat (v. 20). The space formed by the over-arching wings above, the mercy seat below, and by the cherub on the one hand and the cherub on the other, was filled by the Shekinah, the symbol of God's presence (v. 22). The corresponding space on heathen arks was filled by one of the heathen gods.

The cherubim, from the description in Exodus, do not appear to have resembled, as some suppose, those which Ezekiel beheld in vision. His cherubim were a compound of man, lion, ox, and eagle. All that we know with certainty regarding the tabernacle cherubim is what is said of them in Exodus (25:18–22).

And make two cherubim out of hammered gold at the ends of the cover (Exod. 25:18).

As the holy of holies was a type of heaven, and the ark of God's heavenly throne, we are strongly of opinion, notwithstanding all that has been written to the contrary, that the two golden cherubim standing on the mercy seat, and the cherubim glowing on the roof and on the walls, were symbolical of heaven's bright inhabitants, redeemed men and holy angels. Those on the mercy seat seem specially to indicate the angels. The golden cherubim, as shown in the woodcut, are represented as gazing with the most intense and delighted interest on the blood-sprinkled mercy seat (Exod. 25:20). This is the very attitude of the angels with respect to what that blood signified. With faces eagerly and lovingly bending down on our world, they are ever reading with absorbing and joyful interest the story of the cross as it unfolds itself in the church, in the mission-field, and in the Sabbath-school: "Which things the angels desire to look into" (1 Pet. 1:12; literal translation, "to bend looking").

It was revealed to them that they were not serving themselves but you, when they spoke of the things that have now been told you by those who have preached the gospel to you by the Holy Spirit sent from heaven. Even angels long to look into these things (1 Pet. 1:12).

The Shekinah

was the name given by the Jews to the visible manifestation of God's presence, filling the space between the mercy seat and the overarching wings of the cherubim. "Shine forth, thou that dwellest between the cherubim" (Ps. 80:1). It appears to have been a supernatural brightness or splendor, a very luminous object, resembling a bright cloud or flame. What symbol could be more appropriate of Him of whom it is said, "God is light"?

God Not Represented by a Material Figure

Though the guardians or bearers of God's throne might be represented by figures expressive of their great and noble powers, no human figures or combination of animals in a figure were ever permitted to represent the living and true God. He did, indeed, condescend, in consequence of the inability of the Hebrews to realize the idea of an unseen and spiritual God, to grant them a symbol of His presence, that they might be duly impressed with the grand truth that He, as their God and King, was dwelling in their midst. Nevertheless that symbol was not the likeness of any of His creatures, however significant they might be of power, goodness, love, or other great qualities.

It is not necessary to suppose that Moses or the high priest, when consulting Jehovah, entered the holy of holies. The probability is that Moses, standing while so engaged before the golden altar, would hear the voice of God coming from between the cherubim.

God Speaking from the Ark

There are several recorded instances of God speaking to His servants from the ark. The following are examples:—"And when Moses was gone into the tabernacle of the congregation to speak with Him, then he heard the voice of one speaking unto him from off the mercy seat that was upon the ark of the testimony, from between the two cherubim; and He spake unto him" (Num. 7:89). "And the Lord called unto Moses and spake unto him out of the tabernacle of the congregation" (Lev. 1:1). "Then all the children of Israel, and all the people, went up, and came unto the house of God, and wept, and sat there before the Lord, and fasted that day until even, and offered burnt offerings and peace offerings before the Lord. And the children of Israel inquired of the Lord (for the ark of the covenant of God was there in those days, and Phinehas, the son of Eleazar, the son of Aaron, stood before it in those days) saying, Shall I yet again go out to battle against the children of Benjamin my brother, or shall I cease? And the Lord said, Go up; for to-morrow I will deliver them into thine hand" (Judges 20:26–28). The ark was thus the throne of God, on which He was seated by a visible symbol. The people's representative, the high priest, was permitted to approach, and was favored with an audience. God graciously listened to their petitions, and answered in an audible voice.

The mercy seat with the cherubim, as already noticed, was not simply the lid, but an object distinct from the ark. Yet the two were comprehended in the general name, "The Ark." Both together formed the divine throne. Here God in visible symbol was enthroned.

Veneration in Which the Ark Was Held

From the first the ark was regarded as the most sacred vessel connected with the tabernacle, and

When the camp is to move, Aaron and his sons are to go in and take down the shielding curtain and cover the ark of the Testimony with it. Then they are to cover this with hides of sea cows, spread a cloth of solid blue over that and put the poles in place (Num. 4:5-6).

But God struck down some of the men of Beth Shemesh, putting seventy of them to death because they had looked into the ark of the LORD. The people mourned because of the heavy blow the LORD had dealt them, and the men of Beth Shemesh asked, "Who can stand in the presence of the LORD, this holy God? To whom will the ark go up from here?" Then they sent messengers to the people of Kiriath Jearim, saying, "The Philistines have returned the ark of the LORD. Come down and take it up to your place" (1 Sam. 6:19–21).

circumstances occurred during its history to increase the veneration in which it was held. We have already seen that in the instructions given by God to Moses concerning the tabernacle it had the foremost place, being described before the rest of the sacred furniture, and even before the sanctuary itself. It stood in the most holy place, a chamber no one ever entered, save the high priest, and he only on one day of the year. When carried from place to place in the wilderness, it was hid from mortal gaze by a covering (Num. 4:5, 6). It was death for any one to touch it, or even to look into it (Num. 4:15). None but those divinely appointed were permitted to carry it (Num. 4:15). The Levites, to whom the duty pertained, lifted up the ark on their shoulders, and marched in the forefront of the army, leading the way, guided by the cloudy pillar moving in the air above them (Num. 10:33–36). The ark was thus the standard of the moving host, and not only led the way, but went before to search out a resting-place for the wanderers (Num. 10:33). The various encampments were fixed by it. After reaching the Holy Land, it was set up at Gilgal (Josh. 5:10), and afterward was removed to Shiloh (Josh. 18:1), where it remained for three or four hundred years. It was for some time in the possession of the Philistines (1 Sam. 4:11). It was removed by David to Mount Zion when he fixed his residence there (2 Sam. 6:12–16), and at last found a resting-place in the temple of Solomon (2 Chron. 5:5).

The Power of the Ark

Many striking instances attest its great sacredness and mighty power. Many of the people of Bethshemesh were smitten dead for looking into it (1 Sam. 6:19–21). It overthrew Dagon, the god of the Philistines, in his own temple (1 Sam. 5:3–5). It parted the waves of the Jordan, and made a dry way for the many thousands of Israel to pass over, and was upheld in the middle of that hitherto untrodden path until all Israel stood safe on the shores of the promised land. And before it the proud walls of Jericho fell down. These proofs of its power could not fail to keep alive and increase the veneration with which it was regarded.

Typical and Spiritual Significance

The two tables of stone, with the ten command-ments written on them with the finger of God, were the principal deposits the ark contained. These are the twin-pillars supporting the moral government of God. They remind us that righteousness and truth are the foundation of God's throne, attributes from which fallen man can look for nothing but condem-nation. But blessed be God, the mercy seat is sprin-kled with blood, and that speaks of mercy. Righteousness and truth are still, as they ever shall be, the foundation of God's throne, and the awful voice we hear from it today is, "The soul that sinneth it shall die." But oh, forever praise the Lord! The eye of faith beholds that on the mercy seat which pacifies the troubled conscience. Blood on the mercy seat? Yes, and the only blood that can atone for sin. Christ, our great high priest, has entered the true holy of holies, and, with His own precious blood, sprinkled yonder mercy seat, so that the greatest transgressor may now approach the throne without dismay, and there obtain the forgiveness of all his sins.

Look again at the ark, it was

The Meeting-Place for God and the Israelites

Here the high priest, who represented the people, met God, and for himself and them obtained forgive-ness of sin, and in case of doubt and difficulty received directions, in an audible voice, to guide them in the path of duty. It was on account of what the blood (sprinkled on the Propitiatory) prefigured, that God and sinful men could meet before the gold-en throne. Christ Jesus is now the true propitiatory, and here, and nowhere else, can God and sinners meet. If we seek God here we will find Him, and find Him ever ready to hear and answer our petitions, and to do "exceeding abundantly above all that we ask or think." Have you met God here? Do you come daily in faith to this mercy seat, and cry for pardon of your sins, grace to help you in time of need, and light to guide you in the way that you should go? Remember, if you continue at a distance from the meeting-place, while your day of grace lasts, on the day of judgment, when Christ will be seated on the great white throne, you will find yourself on the left hand of the Judge, and hear these awful words addressed to you, "Depart from me, ye cursed, into everlasting fire, prepared for the devil and his angels."

Therefore go and make disciples of all the nations, baptizing them in the name of the Father and of the Son and of the Holy Spirit, and teaching them to obey everything I have commanded you. And surely I am with you always, to the very end of the age (Matt. 28:19, 20).

Look once more at the ark of the covenant. God, seated on this golden throne, dwelt in the midst of Israel, and through the medium of the high priest held fellowship with them. "Here," He said, "I will commune with thee."

The mystic flame, the symbol of the Divine presence, was one of the peculiar privileges of God's ancient people: to them, and to them only, pertained the glory. It is true the Shekinah was seen by no one save the high priest, and by him, as we have seen, on only one day of the year, but part of the mystic flame penetrating through the roof of the tabernacle, was enshrined in the cloudy pillar that rested on the roof of the sacred tent when the Israelites were encamped, and moved in the air right above the ark when it was carried in the wilderness by the Levites, so that in the fiery cloudy pillar the Israelites ever had a visible symbol of God's presence in their midst. God's people in our day are not favored with a visible symbol of His presence. Are their privileges less than those of God's ancient people? By no means; they are infinitely greater, for the darkness of types and shadows has passed away, and the true light now shineth: the moon of the Old Testament has arisen, the glorious sun of the New. Though unseen by bodily eye, God is still present in the assembly of His saints, and not in a few selected places as of old—in tabernacle or temple —but wherever they meet to seek His face, glad with His gracious presence. Genuine believers, few or many, when they meet together in Jesus' name, realize the fulfillment of the gracious promise, "In all places where I record My name I will come unto thee, and I will bless thee" (Exod. 20:24), and "Lo, I am with you always" (Matt. 28:20).

Places that are consecrated by the presence of Him who loved the church and gave Himself for it, do not require to be sprinkled with so-called holy water by popish or ritualistic priests in order to secure His gracious presence.

Jesus, where'er Thy people meet,
There they behold Thy mercy seat,
Where'er they seek Thee, Thou art found,
And every place is holy ground.

Priest.
*The above from former editions, supposed to have been embroidered
with needlework. See illustration (p. 90) of priest executed for this edition
to illustrate the text, "Thou shalt weave the coat in chequer work,"
Exod. 28:1–43 (RV).*

16
THE PRIESTS

After the giving of the law, the office of priest was restricted to one family, that of Aaron: "Take unto thee Aaron thy brother, and his sons with him, from among the children of Israel, that he may minister unto Me in the priest's office, even Aaron, Nadab, and Abihu, Eleazar, and Ithamar, Aaron's sons" (Exod. 28:1).

Qualifications

Every applicant for the priesthood had to prove his descent from Aaron, and was required to be free from bodily defect or blemish. An Israelite, for example —who had a flat nose, or who was broken-footed, broken-handed, or crook-backed, or who had married a profane woman or one who had been put away from her husband—was not permitted to discharge sacerdotal duties, even though he belonged to the illustrious house of Aaron (Lev. 21): "He shall not go in unto the veil, nor come nigh unto the altar" (v. 23). Exclusion from the priest's office, because of these and similar physical and moral disqualifications, pointed to the dignity and holy character of the position occupied by a priest, and to the inward purity requisite for the proper discharge of his sacred duties.

Duties

The chief duty of the priests was to offer or present offerings and sacrifices to God. Sometimes they had to kill the victims (Lev. 16:11) and always to sprinkle and pour out their blood, and burn their

Aaron shall bring the bull for his own sin offering to make atonement for himself and his household, and he is to slaughter the bull for his own sin offering (Lev. 16:11).

carcasses, or part of them, on the altar. They had charge of the altar and the sanctuary: they had to see that the fire was ever burning on the altar: they made loaves of shewbread, trimmed and lit the lamps of the golden candlestick, and evening and morning burned incense on the golden altar, and in general, conducted the sacred services of the tabernacle worship. Their duties were not, however, confined to the performance of the rites and ceremonies of that worship; for the law being committed to their custody, they, with the Levites, were entrusted with the religious instruction of the nation: "He shall teach Jacob Thy judgments, and Israel Thy law" (Deut. 33:10); and the people were exhorted to seek knowledge at the priests' lips.

The priests, however, were too few to skin all the burnt offerings; so their kinsmen the Levites helped them until the task was finished and until other priests had been consecrated, for the Levites had been more conscientious in consecrating themselves than the priests had been (2 Chron. 29:34).

The whole tribe of Levi was given to the priests for the purpose of assisting them in their sacred work. The Levite, unless in an emergency, was not permitted to perform any strictly priestly act. He could not offer up the sacrifices, pour out or sprinkle the blood, or burn incense on the golden altar; he could nevertheless do much as the servant of the priest, in assisting him in his multifarious duties. It appears that he could even officiate as a priest should the priests at any time be too few in number to overtake their peculiar duties (2 Chron. 29:34).

Maintenance

The priests were not permitted to follow any secular calling. Their time was entirely devoted to their sacred work; hence it was necessary and just that their maintenance should be provided for at the expense of those for whose spiritual and temporal welfare they ministered. The remuneration consisted principally of the redemption money paid for the first-born Israelites, the first-fruits of the field, the fruit of trees in the fourth year, parts of various of the offerings, and a tenth of the tithes which fell to the Levites. They were not able, of course, to reap all these dues till they reached the promised land. To the tribe of Levi, including the priests, were assigned forty-eight cities (Josh. 21:41).

The towns of the Levites in the territory held by the Israelites were forty-eight in all, together with their pasturelands (Josh. 21:41).

17
THE GARMENTS FOR GLORY AND BEAUTY

The dress of the high priest consisted of eight articles—the breeches, the coat, the girdle, the bonnet, the blue robe, the ephod, the breast-plate, and the mitre (Exod. 28). With the exception of the breeches, all the other garments were in whole or in part visible to the eye of the onlooker. Thus, although the blue robe was worn over the coat and the girdle, the sleeves of the coat with part of its skirt and the ends of the girdle were seen by the observer; and although the ephod was worn over the blue robe, the greater part of the robe, with its splendid fringe of golden bells and pomegranates, was exposed to view; and although the breastplate was worn over the ephod, the greater part of the ephod, with its shoulder-pieces and onyx stones, was conspicuous; while the breast-plate and the mitre without any covering were seen in their entirety by the admiring spectator.

Make sacred garments for your brother Aaron, to give him dignity and honor (Exod. 28:2).

These are the garments they are to make: a breast-piece, an ephod, a robe, a woven tunic, a turban and a sash. They are to make these sacred garments for your brother Aaron and his sons, so they may serve me as priests (Exod. 28:4).

The priestly robes were far more splendid than some people are apt to suppose. Their great costliness and exceeding loveliness is indicated in the Scripture account of them: "They were," we are told, "for glory and for beauty." Yet in these respects we have no doubt they may have been surpassed and outshone by the costume of some heathen priests and eastern potentates. What distinguishes and differentiates the robes of the Jewish high priest from the most gorgeous attire ever worn by earthly grandees, is their spiritual significance. No words of ours could give such emphasis to this truth as the word that appears shining on the mitre, "Holy to the Lord," and which crowning

Make tunics, sashes and headbands for Aaron's sons, to give them dignity and honor (Exod. 28:40).

Make linen undergarments as a covering for the body, reaching from the waist to the thigh (Exod. 28:42).

High Priest.
The above from former editions. The embroidery work supposed to be
executed by needlework. See illustration (p. 94) of the High Priest to
illustrate the text, "Thou shalt weave the coat in chequer work,"
Exod. 28:1–43 (RV)

ornament of the priestly dress with its beautiful inscription, gives its character to all the other articles of attire, so that they are appropriately called "holy garments." Two things about the spiritual significance of these robes we wish you to bear in mind while we speak of the vestments in detail: (1) the high priest arrayed in the garments for glory and for beauty is the grandest of all the types of Jesus, our great high priest; and (2) the garments, in one word, so that you may not forget but remember it as we proceed, symbolize the *livery* we must wear if we would walk in the light of God's countenance on earth, and dwell hereafter and for ever in heaven His dwelling-place.

Make a plate of pure gold and engrave on it as on a seal: HOLY TO THE LORD. Fasten a blue cord to it to attach it to the turban; it is to be on the front of the turban (Exod. 28:36–37).

The whole of the twenty-eighth chapter of Exodus, containing no fewer than forty-three verses, is taken up with the divine directions given to Moses for the making of the priests' robes, and no fewer than thirty-one verses of the thirty-ninth chapter are occupied with an account of the making of them, showing, without doubt, of what great importance He, whose servants the priests were, regarded the garments "for glory and for beauty" with which they were to be attired.

For Aaron and his sons, they made tunics of fine linen—the work of a weaver—and the turban of fine linen, the linen headbands and the under-garments of finely twisted linen. The sash was of finely twisted linen and blue, purple and scarlet yarn—the work of an embroiderer—as the LORD commanded Moses (Exod. 39:27–29).

The white robes, consisting of the breeches, the coat, the girdle, and the bonnet (Exod. 39:27–29), were worn by all the priests; in addition, the high priest wore over them the brighter and colored vestments peculiar to his office.

The breeches, a kind of short drawers made of fine twined linen, reached from "the loins even to the thighs." The purpose they served is referred to in the text (Exod. 28:42). There can be no doubt that like the other articles of white attire, they were emblematic of sanctity (Rev. 19:8), and, in their case more especially, of chastity, and should ever have been reminding their wearers that they could not discharge their sacred duties, so as to please God, unless all impure thoughts were banished from the mind and all carnal desires from the heart. Had the sons of Eli given due heed to the warning voice of this covering, they had not been the means, by committing the sin of fornication, of breaking the neck of their aged father, and

*Fine linen, bright and clean,
was given her to wear
(Fine linen stands for the righteous acts of the saints.) (Rev. 19:8).*

Priest.
From our life-size model.
*To illustrate the text, Exod. 28:39, "And thou shalt weave
the coat in chequer work"* (RV).

of bringing upon themselves a dishonored and untimely death (1 Sam. 3:12–14; 4:11–18). May we ourselves be ever mindful of the warning, and ever ready to give due heed to all incentives to holiness.

The coat, made of fine linen (Heb. "sesh"), so very fine as to somewhat resemble silk, was a gown with sleeves, reaching from the neck to the feet, and was the work of the weaver; not the mere cloth, but the robe itself being woven in the loom (Exod. 39:27). The Egyptians, with whose arts the Hebrews were well acquainted, knew and practiced the weaving of whole garments. The coat was a seamless garment, like that worn by our Savior on the night of His crucifixion, "Woven from the top throughout" (John 19:23).

In the Authorized Version it is spoken of as being broidered. The text in Hebrew, however, does not indicate to embroider, but to weave in squares. The Revised Version gives, perhaps, the best rendering of the original, "to weave in chequer work" (Exod. 28:39); see illustration, p. 90.

The dress being entirely white, was a meet symbol of the entire and spotless purity of our great high priest, and might well have reminded those who typified Him of the sacred nature of their calling, and of the necessity of their hearts being pure, as well as their coats white, if they would please and honor Him whom they served.

Some are of opinion that the coat and girdle for Aaron's sons, being spoken of separately (Exod. 28:40), were not of the same design as those of the high priest (v. 39), but plainer, and without any ornamental work of any kind; but seeing it is stated that they, as well as those for the high priest, were for glory and for beauty (v. 40), and are sometimes spoken of together, "And they made coats of fine linen for Aaron and his sons, and goodly bonnets of fine linen" (Exod. 39:27, 28), we are of opinion that they were identical.

The girdle, we are told in the Authorized Version, was made of needlework (Exod. 28:39), and in Exod. 39:29, it is called "a girdle of fine twined linen, and blue, and purple, and scarlet, of needlework."

For I told him that I would judge his family forever because of the sin he knew about; his sons made themselves contemptible, and he failed to restrain them (1 Sam. 3:13).

The man who brought the news replied, "Israel fled before the Philistines, and the army has suffered heavy losses. Also your two sons, Hophni and Phinehas, are dead, and the ark of God has been captured." When he mentioned the ark of God, Eli fell backward off his chair by the side of the gate. His neck was broken and he died, for he was an old man and heavy. He had led Israel forty years (1 Sam. 4:17–18).

Weave the tunic of fine linen and make the turban of fine linen. The sash is to be the work of an embroiderer (Exod. 28:39).

This vestment . . . is girded to the breast a little above the elbows, by a girdle often going round, four fingers broad, but so loosely woven, that you would think it were the skin of a serpent. It is embroidered with flowers of scarlet, and purple, and blue, and fine twined linen . . . (Josephus, Antiquities 3.7,2).

These texts would lead us to understand that at least the ornamental work of this article of attire was executed with the needle, but this by no means is the case, for "needlework" does not appear in the original. The rendering of Exod. 28:39, in the Revised Version, is, "thou shalt make a girdle, the work of the embroiderer;" and so with respect to Exod. 39:29. In the Variorum Bible we have perhaps a still better rendering: "the work of the variegator." Such work may be executed either by the needle or the loom. The girdle, like the rest of the sacred garments, was undoubtedly the work of the weaver. According to Josephus (*Antiquities* 3.7,2), the girdle, worn by the priests of his day, was four fingers broad, and wound several times round the body at the waist, where it was tied, and hung down to the ankles when the wearer was not engaged in the more weighty duties of his office, as so worn it appeared to most advantage; but when employed in the more laborious services of his calling, such as the offering of sacrifices, he threw it over his left shoulder, so that he might not be impeded by it in the execution of his sacred work. The girdle, an article of eastern dress, bound the loose garments to the body, and seems to have held up the skirt when the wearer was engaged in walking and running, or other exercise, that it might not be in his way, and hence the phrase "to gird the loins." From this circumstance, it became an emblem of readiness for work or duty, and faithfulness in its execution. The girdle was well calculated to impress the priests with a sense of the necessity of their ever being in a state of readiness to perform the rites of their sacred calling, and to remove all such obstacles out of the way as might in the least hinder them in their ministrations.

The aim of every Christian worker should be to be thus girded, and if he is, his girdle will be transcendently beautiful, even lovely beyond compare, like that of our great high priest, "Righteousness shall be the girdle of his loins, and faithfulness the girdle of his reins" (Isa. 11:5).

The bonnet.—The bonnets of the common priests must have had a fine and attractive appearance, being called "goodly bonnets" (Exod. 39:28). In the Revised Version they are called headtires. Josephus describes the bonnets worn by the priests of his day, and probably those of Aaron's sons were similar, or at least somewhat resembled them. "Bands," he says, "or swaths of linen, wound round several times and sewed together, and shaped so as to fit close to the head, that they might not easily fall off." In shape they resembled a crown.

He is to put on the sacred linen tunic, with linen undergarments next to his body; he is to tie the linen sash around him and put on the linen turban. These are sacred garments; so he must bathe himself with water before he puts them on (Lev. 16:4).

The head as well as the rest of the body of the priest being clothed in white, may have been intended to teach him that in exercising his office, he should have aimed at the entire consecration of his body, as well as all the faculties of his mind, of which the head is the temple. The white bonnet should ever have been reminding him that it was necessary to the due execution of the duties of his office, that he exercise the mind with holy thoughts, and thus effectually guard it against the entrance of evil thoughts. May it be ours so to exercise our minds.

The breeches, coat, girdle, and bonnet formed the official costume of the ordinary priests, and had a comely and lovely appearance, the coat being beautifully woven in chequer work, and the girdle shining resplendently with bright colors, the goodly bonnet crowning the whole. The white robes, as well as the more gorgeously colored ones of the high priest, were "for glory and for beauty" (Exod. 28:40). He whom the white-robed priests typified, was holy, harmless, undefiled, and separate from sinners. He offered Himself without spot to God. Those whom He has made a kingdom of priests are said to be arrayed in fine linen, clean and white, which is the righteousness of saints (Rev. 19:8). John, in his vision of heaven, saw a great multitude which no man could number, "clothed with white robes, and palms in their hands" (Rev. 7:9). From these and other allusions in the book of Revelation to saints being clothed in white raiment, and also to numerous other passages of Scripture, in which white is employed as an emblem of purity, it is apparent that the white robes of the priests were emblematic of sanctity. Their name, "holy garments"

High Priest.
From our life-size model of the High Priest.
To illustrate the text, Exod. 28:1–43, "Thou shalt weave the coat
in chequer work" (RV)

(Lev. 16:4), seems to confirm this view. They should ever have been reminding their wearers of that inward holiness, without which they could not serve God acceptably.

The days of symbolism having passed away, gospel ministers are not required to array themselves in white robes. It is a matter of no moment whatever, whether, when they enter the pulpit, they appear in a white gown, or a blue gown, or a red gown, or a black gown, or no gown at all. If, however, they and those to whom they minister, would serve and worship God so as to please and honor Him, they must be possessed of that heart purity of which these robes were expressive: "Who shall ascend into the hill of the Lord? Or who shall stand in His holy place? He that hath clean hands, and a pure heart" (Ps. 24:3, 4).

He who has clean hands and a pure heart, who does not lift up his soul to an idol or swear by what is false (Ps. 24:4).

The colored garments worn by the high priest over the white robes consisted of the blue robe, the ephod, the girdle of the ephod, the breastplate, and the mitre (see priest, p. 96).

They made the robe of the ephod entirely of blue cloth—the work of a weaver— (Exod. 39:22).

The blue robe, reaching from the neck to a little below the knees, was one entire piece of woven work (Exod. 39:22), "all of blue" (v. 22), both warp and weft consisting of fine blue dyed linen yarn. As it had not sleeves, there were arm slits at the sides. And in the midst at the top of the dress, was an aperture, large enough for the passage of the head. Around the inner rim of this hole was an ornamental border of woven work, "as it were the hole of a habergeon" ("coat of mail," RV), "that it be not rent" (Exod. 28:32).

The gold bells and the pomegranates are to alternate around the hem of the robe (Exod. 28:34).

Gold bells and pomegranates.—Along the hem of the skirt was a very rich and splendid ornamental fringe, of golden bells, and tassels in the form of pomegranates, made of blue, and of purple, and of scarlet yarn (Exod. 28:33–35), a golden bell and a pomegranate alternating (v. 34). There was thus a bell between every two pomegranates, and a pomegranate between every two bells.

The Sounding of the Bells

When the high priest moved, the bells made a tinkling sound, and this was intended—"his sound shall be heard when he goeth into the holy place before the Lord, and when he cometh out that he die not."

The significance of this sound being heard is not clearly indicated. Some are of opinion that it was to indicate to worshippers without, the exact time when the high priest was engaged in offering up incense, and presenting prayer to God, so that they might mingle their prayers with his. Such a sound, however, as the bells were capable of making could not be heard by the people. Besides, it was *not* while he was *standing* and engaged at the golden altar that the bells sounded: It was *while* he was *walking* (Exod. 28:35).

Rhind (*The High Priest of Israel*, p. ii) is of opinion that the sound of the bells symbolized praise. He says:—"It was impossible for the high priest to minister before the Lord in the holy place without praise. It is said in Psalm 50:23, 'Whoso offereth praise glorifieth Me,' and this, he says, explains the difficulty of the passage in Exod. 28:35, 'that he die not.' When Aaron stood at the golden altar, and sweet fragrance of incense went up before the Lord, and his hands were lifted up on high, the golden bells sent forth their sweet melody (?) and praise went up to God for the privilege of prayer and intercession." All this is very beautifully put and sounds well, but Mr. Rhind seems to forget that it was not when the high priest was standing officiating at the golden altar, but "as *he went*" (Ecclesiasticus 14:10, 11), or as *he was walking into and from the holy place* (Exod. 28:35) that the bells were sounding.

Not much further light is to be got from the passage in Ecclesiasticus, "He compassed him about with many bells of gold all round about, that as he went (not stood) there might be a sound and a noise made that he might be heard in the temple for a memorial to the children of his people." "Be heard," certainly not by the people without, who were at too great a distance to hear the sound of the bells, but by God. Of course, it was as representing the Israelites that the high priest ministered in the temple.

Our opinion is that the sound of the bells was intended to intimate to Israel's God the high priest's entrance into and his withdrawal from, the sanctuary, as it would have been deemed irreverent in him to approach or depart from the sacred precincts, God's dwelling-place, without thus giving notice. Besides, the sound indicated that he was attired in the robes of his office, and thus duly qualified for performing his sacred calling in the holy place.

The Symbolism of the Blue Robe

The gown was all white, the covering robe all blue. The white gown was an emblem of heart purity or negative holiness, as distinguished from the exercise of holiness, and the fruit it yields. The blue robe was an emblem of active holiness, as exhibited in the fruits of righteousness and the gifts and graces which should adorn the child of God. The pomegranates around the hem of the skirt favor this view. Along with the celestial blue of the robe, they seemed quietly and winsomely inviting their wearers, and us through them, to abound in the fruits of righteousness.

The high priest was reminded by the blue robe that, not only heart purity, but active virtue was looked for in a high degree in him, and that he should constantly have been aiming and striving after heavenly attainments.

Jesus our great high priest, was not only spotlessly pure, but His whole life was adorned, as that of no mere man's ever was, by good words and good deeds.

That the beautiful heavenly blue of the robe was emblematic of active holiness is no mere fancy or conceit of ours. It is God Himself who tells us what the blue was intended so impressively to symbolize and teach: "And the Lord spake unto Moses, saying, Speak unto the children of Israel, and bid them, that they make them fringes on the borders of their garments, through their generations, and that they put upon the fringe of each border *a cord of blue:* and it shall be unto you for a fringe, that ye may look upon it, and *remember* all the commandments of the Lord and *do them*" (Num. 15:37–40, RV). If a mere blue cord or ribbon had this significance, how much more an entire blue robe.

We ourselves might not be the worse of ever remembering what the white and the blue so impressively taught. When we gaze up at the stainless white clouds floating serenely in the air above us, may we ever hear the voice of God saying through them to us, "Be ye holy, for I am holy," and when we look beyond to the robe that covers them, the vast blue dome of the heavens, may we ever hear the voice of God through the blue, saying unto us, "Remember all the commandments of the Lord, and do them."

ON THE RIGHT SHOULDER ONYX STONE.

The Names of Jacob's Six Eldest Sons, "According to Their Birth."

1. Reuben.
2. Simeon.
3. Levi.
4. Judah.
5. Dan.
6. Naphtali.

ON THE LEFT SHOULDER ONYX STONE.

The Names of Jacob's Six Youngest Sons, "According to Their Birth."

7. Gad.
8. Asher.
9. Issachar.
10. Zebulon.
11. Joseph.
12. Benjamin.

References to the above, p. 99.

The ephod and its girdle.—The ephod, reaching from the shoulders to a little above the knees, consisted of two equal parts: one for the front and one for the back, and these two were united at the shoulders by

Shoulder-pieces, whose ends were joined to the corresponding ends of the ephod (Exod. 39:4, RV).

The material they were made of is not mentioned, and we take it for granted that it was the same rich cloth as that of the ephod itself.

The material of the ephod, a very rich and splendid vestment, was made of gold; and of blue, purple, and scarlet yarn, and fine twined undyed linen (Exod. 39:2). "They," we are told, "beat the gold into thin plates, and cut it into wires, to work in the dyed and undyed linen."

The work of the weaver.—The ephod was woven in the loom by "the cunning workmen," that is by the skillful artificers. The ornamentation probably consisted of figures of flowers, and other lovely devices.

They made shoulder pieces for the ephod, which were attached to two of its corners, so it could be fastened (Exod. 39:4).

The Two Onyx Stones

Two large and magnificent onyx stones, "set" (or enclosed, RV) in ouches or sockets, of gold, were placed on the shoulder-pieces. How the stones, by their ouches, were fixed to the shoulder-pieces, to which they must have been very firmly bound, we are not told.

Take two onyx stones and engrave on them the names of the sons of Israel (Exod. 28:9).

The names of the sons of Jacob, were engraved on the stones, "with the work of an engraver, like the engravings of a signet" (Exod. 28:6–12). The six eldest sons on the stone that rested on the right shoulder, and the other six on the stone that rested on the left shoulder "according to their birth" (v. 10). (See illustration, p. 98.)

The stones with the names on them, conspicuously and emphatically showed that the high priest was the representative of all the children of Israel as he ministered before the Lord in the sanctuary. "And thou," we are told, "shalt put the stones upon the shoulder-pieces of the ephod, to be stones of memorial for the children of Israel. And Aaron shall bear their names before the Lord for a memorial" (Exod. 28:12); so that it should ever be kept in remembrance while ministering before the Lord that He was the people's substitute acting for and in their stead.

The girdle (or *band,* RV) *of the ephod* was of the same material as that of the ephod itself (Exod. 39:5), and seems to have formed a part of either the front or back part of the ephod. The use it served was to gird or bind the ephod, both before and behind, close to the body.

In the Authorized Version it is called the curious girdle of the ephod, but there seems no reason why it should be so named, seeing that the ephod itself was made of identical material and is not so designated. The original does not indicate curious, but rather skillfully formed, which agrees with the rendering of the Revised Version, "And the cunningly woven band that was upon it, to gird it withal, was of the same piece, and the like work thereof" (Exod. 39:5).

The Chief Design of the Ephod

appears to have been to bear up the onyx stones. The high priest, who was charged with the interests of all the tribes by having these stones, with the twelve names of the children of Israel engraved on them, upon his shoulders, very significantly, though figuratively, bore the people on his shoulders. He was constantly reminded by the precious gems, that it was his duty to care for the children of Israel and strive after their welfare. The situation of the stones may also, on account of its conspicuousness, have been meant to render the jewels easily seen by all within view of the high priest.

The shoulders are distinguished by strength or bearing power, and hence they became an emblem of rule. Thus it is said of Eliakim, "And the key of the house of David will I put upon his shoulder, so he shall open, and none shall shut, and he shall shut and none shall open" (Isa. 22:22). Of our Great high priest, charged with all the interests of His people, it was said, "The government shall be upon his shoulders" (Isa. 9:6). True believers by faith may now behold Jesus at the right hand of the Majesty in the heavens, and discern that He cares for them, yea, they may read their very names deep graven on the palms of His hands (Isa. 49:16). Every breath of the Holy Spirit that is breathed upon their souls is a fresh token that the great Intercessor is attending to their interests.

If you are a child of God, you may well rejoice when you ponder the precious truth that the Great high priest bears you on His shoulders and that, however many and weighty your varied interests may be, His strength can never fail, for He is an almighty friend. No load is too heavy for Him to bear. Remember, however, that if you would benefit by His mediation, you must ever keep looking to Him as your only Priest and Savior, and ever be rolling all the burden of your soul over on Him. He invites you to do so, will not be pleased with you unless you comply. "Come unto Me, all ye that labor and are heavy laden, and I will give you rest."

There are cares, however, which gospel ministers, and other servants of the Lord, cannot get quit of by casting them on Jesus Christ. He may help them by His grace to bear them, but cannot ease them of the burden. Metaphorically they have, like the high priest of old, to bear those committed to their trust on their shoulders, otherwise they cannot be true shepherds of the flock. The life of a true and faithful pastor is no sinecure: it is not one of ease. Those who think so are not fit for the office, and if they enter on the ministry, they are sure to dishonor, and not to magnify, their calling. No occupation calls for more carefulness in counting the cost before choosing it than that of the Christian ministry.

The members of a congregation may be too numerous for the minister to have every individual at all times on his mind, and in that case it is only in a very general way he can care for them, but even what that involves is a heavy load, which only those who have experienced it know. And then as individual cases arise, requiring his special attention, he cannot shrink, without disloyalty to his Lord and Master, from trying, as far as he is able, to bear the burden. Burden-bearing, however, is not without its compensation. Earth's greatest Burden-bearer is now heaven's greatest rejoicer. And those Gospel pastors who have borne most of the heat and burden of the ministerial

Fashion a breastpiece for making decisions—the work of a skilled craftsman. Make it like the ephod: of gold, and of blue, purple and scarlet yarn, and of finely twisted linen (Exod. 28:15).

day, will be among the happiest of heaven's bright inhabitants.

What we have said about gospel ministers is also true, although it may be in a lesser degree, of Sabbath-school teachers, parents, and others who as professing Christians have the spiritual well-being of others to care for. We may go a step further and say, that no true Christian can be altogether freed from burden bearing, or can be so situated that there is no one who has not claims of some kind or another as the Master. See, then, that you bear "one another's burdens, and so fulfill the law of Christ."

Forget not the onyx stones, with the names of the sons of Jacob engraved on them, borne on the shoulders of the high priest, and their spiritual significance.

The Breastplate

was the high priest's outermost article of attire, and worn above the ephod to which it was so closely bound that the two appeared to form but one resplendent whole. It was four square, one span (nine inches) long, and one broad (Exod. 28:15–30; 39:8–21). The cloth was double (see p. 104), either to render the breastplate sufficiently strong to bear the gems set in it, or as some suppose that it might be a bag or pouch to hold the Urim and Thummim. It was made of the same rich and bright material as the ephod, and like it was the work of the skillful weaver; shining radiantly all over with gold, blue, purple and scarlet, it formed a most beautiful and appropriate groundwork for the lovely and exceedingly precious and brilliant gems set in it.

Then mount four rows of precious stones on it. In the first row there shall be a ruby, a topaz and a beryl; in the second row a turquoise, a sapphire and an emerald; in the third row a jacinth, an agate and an amethyst; in the fourth row a chrysolite, an onyx and a jasper. Mount them in gold filigree settings (Exod. 28:17–20).

The twelve precious stones set in this beautiful breastplate were settings of stone (Exod. 28:17), "enclosed in ouches (or sockets) of gold in their settings" (Exod. 39:13, RV) "even four rows of stones" (Exod. 28:17), as follows:—

NAMES ON THE TWELVE STONES.

First Row.			
b Carbuncle. Zebulon. 3.	Topaz. Issachar. 2.	*a* Sardius. Judah. 1.	First Row.
Second Row.			
d Diamond. Gad. 6.	Sapphire. Simeon. 5.	*c* Emerald. Reuben. 4.	Second Row.
Third Row.			
Amethyst. Benjamin. 9.	Agate. Manasseh. 8.	*e* Ligure. Ephraim. 7.	Third Row.
Fourth Row.			
Jasper. Naphtali. 12.	Onyx. Asher. 11.	*f* Beryl. Dan. 10.	Fourth Row.

Scale—3 inches to 9 inches.

c, or Carbuncle.	*b*, or Emerald.	*a*, or Ruby.
f, or Chalcedony.	*e*, or Jacinth.	*d*, or Sardine.

The names of the twelve sons of Jacob, and arranged according to their birth (Exod. 28:10). The names, however, on the breastplate were those of the twelve tribes, each stone bearing the name of one of the tribes, and arranged, not as in the case of the ephod according to age, but according to the order of the tribes (Exod. 39:14). The names of Levi and Joseph are not included in those of the tribes; but the names of Joseph's two sons—Manasseh and Ephraim—are, thus making the number of the tribes twelve, the same as that of the number of the sons of Jacob.

The Breastplate over the High Priest's Heart

The breastplate bearing the precious stones was placed over the high priest's heart, and kept in its position by means of two chains like cords of wreathen work of pure gold. The under ends of the chains were put on two gold rings which were attached to the upper corners of the breastplate (see woodcut, p. 104), the other two ends of the chains being fixed to the forefront of the two gold ouches that rested on the shoulder-pieces. By this contrivance the breastplate was prevented from moving below its place over the heart, and was prevented from moving above it by means of rings which were placed on the inner edge of the two lower corners of the breastplate (see woodcut, below), and by these rings being bound into corresponding rings on the ephod by a lace of blue, "that it might be above the cunningly woven band of the ephod (which wound round the breast at this place, see woodcut, below), and that the breastplate might not be loosed from the ephod" (Exod. 39:15–21, RV). (See woodcut of high priest, below.)

For the breastpiece they made braided chains of pure gold, like a rope (Exod. 39:15).

Part for folding back.*

Breastplate.
To render the cloth sufficiently strong to bear the precious stones, or, as some suppose, to form a pouch or bag to hold the Urim and Thummim.

Urim and Thummim

Moses was commanded to put into the breastplate the Urim and Thummim (Exod. 28:30). Whatever these were, their names signify light and perfection. Some tell us that they were two small images which God gave to Moses on the Mount. But there is not a word in Scripture to justify this supposition. Others inform us that they were three small stones with "yes" inscribed on one of them, "no" on another, and that the remaining one had no word on it. When the high priest entered the holy place to consult Jehovah, he put the question so as to receive a simple negative or affirmative. Having put a question, he put his hand into the breastplate (which those holding the opinion we are now considering say was open at the top like a bag or pouch). (See woodcut, p. 104.) Should he happen to take out the stone with "yes" on it, "yes" was the answer to his question; if the one with "no," "no" was the reply; and if it should happen to be the blank stone which came to his hand, this was an intimation that he was to receive no answer. This opinion is contrary to scripture, which again and again tells us that the responses were given in an audible voice.

Aaron will always bear the means of making decisions for the Israelites over his heart before the LORD *(Exod. 28:30).*

Another view taken by some writers is, that the twelve gems of the breastplate constituted the Urim and Thummim, and that the responses of Jehovah to the inquiries of the high priest were given by means of the letters of the precious stones intended to spell out the answers becoming supernaturally illuminated. To this opinion it is objected that the Urim and Thummim were things which were put "in" and not "on" the breastplate. This, however, is no valid objection, for the word "in" in the text admits, without the least straining, of being rendered "on." There is this fatal objection, however, that the responses are not in accordance with the Word of God, which, as already observed, says they were given in an audible voice.

We lean to the opinion that the precious stones constituted the Urim and the Thummim, but not by reason of any supernatural illumination of the letters, and that the stones rendered the breastplate the ornament or badge qualifying the high priest to make inquiries of Jehovah. "They shall be upon Aaron's heart when he goeth in before the Lord."

As one purpose to serve by consulting Jehovah was to give righteous decisions in difficult cases, the breastplate is probably on that account called the breastplate of judgment.

It may be noticed here that in the divine directions given to make the various articles of attire

(Exod. 28:2–43), nothing is said as to the making of the Urim and the Thummim, and in the account of the articles of attire being made (Exod. 39:1–31), the Urim and the Thummim are not mentioned, thus going to show that they and the twelve precious stones of the breastplate were identical.

Also put the Urim and the Thummim in the breastpiece, so they may be over Aaron's heart whenever he enters the presence of the LORD. Thus Aaron will always bear the means of making decisions for the Israelites over his heart before the LORD (Exod. 28:30).

The precious stones may have received the collective name of the Urim and Thummim—*First*, on their own account. Of all earthly objects these precious stones are the most lustrous, and emit light of themselves. Like the stars, they shine in the darkest night, and for that reason they have been called the stars of earth. Are they not well called light? Thummim signifies perfection. The stones from their brilliancy, purity, and uncommon beauty are perhaps the most striking emblems which earthly objects furnish of truth or perfection, and are, therefore, not inappropriately named Thummim. *Second,* On account of their being the badge or ornament necessary for the high priest to wear when consulting Jehovah. The object of the high priest was to get light on some dark subject, or to arrive at the truth on some matter he could not discover otherwise, or to give a righteous decision in cases in which his knowledge or wisdom was deficient, and such as would accord with innocence and justice. For this reason the gems seem to be appropriately called "Urim and Thummim." *Third,* On account of their representing the children of Israel. The names of all the tribes being on the stones—one name on each—the Israelites might see in these stones an emblem of what it was designed they should become before they were meet for being worshippers in the heavenly temple; and the high priest might be reminded by them that his mission was to bring the Israelites into that state of perfection.

Like these gems, man by nature is of the earth earthy. Both have their origin in mother earth. Yet both when polished may shine like the stars of the firmament. Every Israelite when he looked upon or thought of these shining gems should have been humbled on account of sin which dimmed the original beauty and luster of his soul, and should have sought by faith in the appropriate means of restoration, the services of the sanctuary, and by constant effort in dependence on divine aid, to have his soul made bright and beautiful like the resplendent stones of the breastplate, and the high priest's constant aim should have been to bring the people into this state of beauty and perfection.

Significance of the Breastplate Being Worn over the Heart

This splendid jeweled ornament being worn right over the high priest's heart reminded him that he was not only to care for the people, as the onyx stones on his shoulders taught him, but also to love them; he was to have a place in his heart as well as on his shoulders for all the tribes of Israel. The Aaronic priests, even the best of them, were not perfect, and were liable at times to fail in their duties both in caring for, and loving, the people. Besides, it was only in a very general way that they could care for and love those to whom they ministered: they could not possibly occupy their minds with every individual Israelite. But believers have a great and perfect high priest. One who never for a single moment can forget any one of them, even the humblest, nor ever cease attending to their individual interest. In all their sorrows, trials, bereavements, sufferings and temptations, He deeply sympathizes, and as no other can. It is a human heart that beats in the bosom of the great high priest, and it is ever beating with warmest affection for all His loved ones.

If the pious Israelite when he saw, or thought of, the name of his tribe glittering on the high priest's breastplate, rejoiced with a glad heart, knowing that in consequence he had an interest in his mediation, how much greater should be the joy of the child of God now, when with the eye of faith he surveys the breast of Jesus, the great high priest, and beholds his name shining there.

> Behold those jewels on His breast,
>> Each as a signet graved,
> Close to that bosom warmly pressed
>> Lie those by Jesus saved.

How greatly it would gladden some of you to have a place, even a small corner in the hearts of some of the best men and women in the world, in that of our Queen for example, but this is beyond our getting. Her heart and theirs are already so overcrowded, that there is no room remaining for us. But in the best of all hearts, the heart of Jesus, of Him who sits upon the throne of the universe, there is no lack of room for us all. That heart has an infinite capacity. Millions and tens of millions are already safely in this blessed haven of rest and peace, and countless millions more down to the end of time will continue to enter in, and there personally experiencing the blessedness of being loved by Jesus will rejoice with joy unspeakable and full of glory.

Blessed truth! There is room for us all. There is room for you if you are not there already. "Him that cometh unto Me I will in no wise cast out," are His own encouraging words. If you remain without, the fault is yours, not His.

Gospel ministers, missionaries, Sabbath-school teachers, parents, and all others who bear Christ's name, like the high priest, are called upon not only *to care for* those committed to their care, but also *to love* them; to have a place for them in their hearts as well as on their shoulders. If they prove themselves followers of their divine pattern, their hearts will beat with warm love and deepest sympathy for those depending on their ministrations.

Let us remember the breastplate over the high priest's heart with the names of the tribes of Israel engraved on the stones inserted in it, and forget not its lessons for ourselves.

The Mitre

The high priest's crowning article of attire, like the goodly bonnets of the ordinary priests, was made of fine white linen (Exod. 39:28), fashioned like theirs, and like theirs somewhat resembling a crown.

Distinguishing characteristic of the mitre.—The high priest's headdress was distinguished from that of the ordinary priest, by a plate of pure gold, called the holy crown, fastened to the forefront of the mitre, with a writing, "Holy to the Lord," engraved on it, "like the engravings of a signet" (Exod. 28:36, RV). A lace of blue was tied upon it, "to fasten it upon the mitre" (v. 37). We are not told how this was effected. Probably there was a small narrow aperture at each extremity of the plate; open end of the blue lace or ribbon being passed through one of these small holes, and led across the back of the plate, and then passed through the other hole. Enough of the ribbon passing through to enable it, along with what was reserved at the other end to pass round the head as often as was necessary, before being tied, to bind the golden crown securely to the mitre. (See woodcuts below).

For Aaron and his sons, they made tunics of fine linen—the work of a weaver—and the turban of fine linen, the linen headbands and the under-garments of finely twisted linen (Exod. 39:27–28).

Another lace of blue.—The lace of blue mentioned in Exodus 28:37, seems not to have been used like the one we have been speaking about to tie the gold plate to the mitre, but for the gold plate to be placed on it (the blue lace). "And thou shalt put it (the gold plate) on a lace of blue that it may be upon the mitre" (Exod. 28:37).

Lace of blue for fastening golden crown on the mitre (Exod. 39:31).

FRONT VIEW

BACK VIEW

The Golden Crown.
From life-size model High Priest.

Josephus, who of course, speaks only of the mitre worn by the high priests of his day, says that above the white linen mitre was another of blue. May this not have been an amplification of the lace of blue on which the golden plate of Aaron's time was placed, and suggested by it?

Appropriate finish to the high priest's attire.— The golden crown, with its inscription, "Holy to the Lord," was a most beautiful and appropriate finish to the "garments for glory and for beauty." Every article of attire uttered the sentiment of that inscription. No words could have excelled them.

The mitre and Aaron's consecration.—At the consecration of Aaron the holy crown is specially mentioned: "And he (that is Moses who acted as priest on the occasion) put the mitre upon his head, and upon the mitre, even upon his forehead, did he put the golden plate, the holy crown; and he poured the anointing oil upon Aaron's head" (Lev. 8:9–12).

Always upon Aaron's head.—It is said (Exod. 28:38) that it (the holy crown) shall be always upon his forehead, that they (the offerings) be accepted before the Lord. It was he (Aaron) who, by learning the crown with the words, "Holy to the Lord," shining on it, as indicating the effect of his mediatorial priestly work, rendered the offerings and services of the Israelites, though not in themselves perfectly free from impurity, acceptable to God.

"Holy to the Lord" described the character of the high priest, at least the character which he should bear. They were of all words those which ever served, the Holy One of Israel, and the sacred nature of his office and of the work he was engaged in. The Israelites as well as the high priest himself, were taught by the words that it was their duty to devote themselves to God by a holy life. It is our duty too. Zechariah the prophet (14:20) foretells a time when such would be the universally holy character of God's people, that everything they possessed, things even of the least value not excluded, would be consecrated and devoted to the Lord. On the very bells of the horses, and on the very pots of the kitchen, would be inscribed in shining letters, "Holy to the Lord." May each of us hasten on that blessed and glorious day, by having "Holy to the Lord" shining on all we say and on all we do. May our persons and our property bear

On that day HOLY TO THE LORD will be inscribed on the bells of the horses, and the cooking pots in the LORD's house will be like the sacred bowls in front of the altar (Zech. 14:20).

the lovely inscription. May our chief end ever be to glorify God.

When we think of the beautiful and significant words glittering on the high priest's mitre, can we forget Him who has given us the best commentary on them when He said, "My meat and My drink is to do the will of Him who sent Me," and whose obedience unto death, even the death of the cross, affords their brightest illustration.

> See Aaron, God's anointed priest,
>   Within the veil appear,
> In robes of mystic meaning dressed,
>   Presenting Israel's prayer.
>
> The plate of gold which crowns his brows,
>   His holiness describes;
> His breast displays, in shining rows,
>   The names of all the tribes.
>
> With the atoning blood he stands
>   Before the mercy seat;
> And clouds of incense from his hands
>   Arise with odor sweet.
>
> Urim and Thummim near his heart,
>   In rich engravings worn,
> The sacred light of truth impart,
>   To teach and to adorn.
>
> Through him the eye of faith descries
>   A greater Priest than he;
> Thus Jesus pleads above the skies,
>   For you, my friends, and me.
>
> He bears the names of all His saints
>   Deep in His heart engraved;
> Attentive to the state and wants
>   Of all His love has saved.
> In Him a holiness complete,
>   Light and perfections shine;
> And wisdom, grace, and glory meet;
>   A Savior all Divine.
>
> The blood, which as a priest He bears
>   For sinners, is His own;
> The incense of His prayers and tears
>   Perfumes the holy throne.

In Him my weary soul has rest,
> Though I am weak and vile;
> I read my name upon His breast,
> And see the Father smile.

The time came when the beggar died and the angels carried him to Abraham's side. The rich man also died and was buried. In hell, where he was in torment, he looked up and saw Abraham far away, with Lazarus by his side (Luke 16:22–23).

We have endeavored throughout this chapter to show that the high priest, arrayed in his official garments, was a striking and instructive type of Jesus, our great high priest, and also that these garments symbolized the spiritual raiment worn by all true believers. Now we close with an illustration, showing very strikingly the perfect blessedness of those who are so clothed and the utter misery of those who are not—an illustration no one who hears it can easily if ever forget. It is the illustration employed by a great preacher, the greatest of all, our blessed Savior. You remember the parable. Dives, who was clothed in purple and fine linen, and fared sumptuously every day, died, leaving all his wealth behind him, and just when he passed out of time into eternity, he found the gates of Paradise barred against him. And why? Because he lacked his riches? No; but because he lacked that livery which all must wear who are permitted to enter the realms of bliss, or remain for ever without. The beggar that lay at his gates died also, leaving all his earthly treasures, consisting of but a bundle of rags, behind him. Happily, some time before this, he discovered that his soul was even more destitute of raiment than his miserable body, not having even a rag to cover it. Naked, he now came to Christ for dress, and his soul was clothed with white robes and the garments for glory and for beauty, the righteousness of the saints. And just when his spirit quitted his poor, vile, worn-out, emaciated body, covered with sores, a voice was heard, in which all the hosts of heaven joined, with one grand, loud, triumphant shout, "Ye gates, doors that do last for aye, be lifted up that Lazarus may enter in!"

18
THE LEVITES

The various duties connected with the tabernacle worship were far too numerous for Aaron and his sons to overtake; even the preparing of the sacrifices for the altar involved an amount of physical labor greatly beyond their strength. It is evident, then, that they required assistance. God might have given them as helps all the first-born sons of the Israelites, in whom, ever since the eventful night in Egypt, when the first-born sons of the Egyptians were smitten dead by the destroying angel and the first-born of the Israelites spared alive, he claimed a peculiar right. In their place, however, He saw meet, as an arrangement having many obvious advantages, to give the priests the whole tribe of Levi (Num. 3:12), to which Moses and Aaron belonged.

I have taken the Levites from among the Israelites in place of the first male offspring of every Israelite woman. The Levites are mine (Num. 3:12).

The tribe of Levi numbered 22,000 (Num. 3:39), the first-born Israelites 22,273 (Num. 3:43), so that they were nearly equal. The 273 first-born sons, in excess of the Levites, were by divine permission redeemed at the rate of five shekels each (Num. 3:46–51). Of the 22,000 Levites, 8580 were qualified by age to enter on the duties of their office (Num. 4:47, 48).

All the men from thirty to fifty years of age who came to do the work of serving and carrying the Tent of Meeting numbered 8,580 (Num. 4:47, 48).

The Levites were solemnly set apart to their office by Aaron. Having shaved their flesh and washed their clothes, they were sprinkled with the water of purifying, and then presented as a national offering to the Lord: the nation's representatives, the elders of the respective tribes, putting their hands upon them, thereby signifying that the people gave the Levites to the Lord in place of the first-born. After being thus transferred to the Lord, the Levites offered two bullocks as sacrifices, one for a sin offering and the other for a burnt offering (Num. 8:5–23).

Whatever assistance the priests might require to enable them to overtake their sacred work, the Levites were ever at hand to render it. Some Biblical critics, such as Colenso, would not be so bold in asserting that it was impossible for Aaron and his sons to do all the work connected with the sacrifices if they had not willfully shut their eyes to this fact. It is true the mere Levite, except in cases of emergency (2 Chron. 29:34), could not offer up the sacrifice, sprinkle the blood, burn incense, or perform other priestly acts. In helping, however, to prepare the victims for the altar, and in numerous other ways, he might lawfully assist in the religious services of the tabernacle.

After the Levites lay their hands on the heads of the bulls, use the one for a sin offering to the LORD and the other for a burnt offering, to make atonement for the Levites (Num. 8:12).

In the wilderness the Levites had the sole charge of taking down and putting up the tabernacle, and of transporting it from one place of encampment to another (Num. 4). At one time the Levites may have been seen busy in the tabernacle court, waiting on the priests, and helping them in their work; at another time, taking down the sacred structure; at another, transporting it and its holy vessels through the wilderness; and at another, rearing it in some new place of encampment. Their duties, however, were not confined to such services as these, for to them, with the priests, the religious instruction of the nation was confided: "They shall teach Jacob Thy judgments and Israel Thy law" (Deut. 33:10). These were among the dying words of Moses, and there are numerous passages of Scripture illustrating them, showing that the Levites as well as the priests taught the people (2 Chron. 17:7–9).

When the children of Israel were settled in the promised land, and the tabernacle was fixed for long periods in the same place, the Levites were relieved of a very burdensome part of their labors—that of transporting the sacred edifice from place to place, so that there was no longer any necessity for them all being in attendance at the house of the Lord; consequently they were formed into divisions, and waited on the priests in turn.

When disengaged at the sanctuary, the Levites resided in the Levitical cities, situated in all the tribal territories, not, however, passing their time in mere recreation, but employing it in divers ways for the moral and spiritual welfare of the people. They read and explained the law, assisted the elders in the different towns in the administration of justice, took charge of the cities of refuge, whither those who had sinned through ignorance fled for safety. Dwelling in the midst of every tribe, they were everywhere at hand to explain the law, instruct the ignorant, comfort the afflicted, shield the innocent, punish the guilty, and generally guide the people in the way in which they should go (Deut. 17:8–12; 32:10).

Charged with so many highly important duties, the Levites must have possessed immense influence, and when animated with the spirit of their office, and with love to God and man, could not fail in maintaining and advancing the best interests of the Kingdom of Israel.

With a view to the transference of the scene of worship, from the tabernacle to the temple, David appointed a new arrangement of the Levites, in which we find that besides assisting the priests in the courts of the Lord's House, and instructing the nation, 4000 served as porters, who had charge of opening and shutting the gates, and of admitting only those who had a right to enter; 4000 served as musicians, and conducted the public praise; and 6000 served as officers and judges (1 Chron. 23).

The Levites had no share in the division of the Holy Land, so that the eleven tribes got one-twelfth more territory among them on that account. Seeing that the Levites got no land, and were not permitted to follow a secular calling, it was not only right and fair, but bare justice that provision should be made for their maintenance. To this tribe (priests included) were assigned forty-eight cities (Josh. 21). Besides these cities, one-tenth of the produce of the whole land was to be given to them (Num. 18:21; Deut. 18:1, 2; Neh. 10:37). By this arrangement the Levites got about the same quantity of the produce of the land as the share of the country that should have fallen to them would have yielded had they participated in the division of Canaan. They were thus saved from the toils of cultivation, the service rendered by the

If cases come before your courts that are too difficult for you to judge-whether bloodshed, lawsuits or assaults—take them to the place the LORD your God will choose. Go to the priests, who are Levites, and to the judge who is in office at that time. Inquire of them and they will give you the verdict (Deut. 17:8–9).

The Levites thirty years old or more were counted, and the total number of men was thirty-eight thousand. David said, "Of these, twenty-four thousand are to supervise the work of the temple of the LORD and six thousand are to be officials and judges. Four thousand are to be gatekeepers and four thousand are to praise the LORD with the musical instruments I have provided for that purpose" (1 Chron. 23:3–5).

other tribes being no more than a fair equivalent for the higher and sacred services rendered by the Levites to the nation.

Many of the priests and Levites performed their duties to God and the Hebrew people so as to glorify Him and benefit them, and thereby "purchased to themselves a good degree." And having, through the shadows of the old dispensation, led many an Israelite to look to the substance—Christ the one great sacrifice —they are now among the saints in glory, and shall shine as the stars for ever and ever. Others of the priests and Levites were not distinguished by that holiness becoming their office; and at the time of our Savior's advent, few, very few, were to be found executing the duties of their office with clean hands and a pure heart. But blessed be God, there were still to be found, even then, some who walked in all the commandments and ordinances of the Lord blameless. With all their sins and shortcomings, the Levites, up to the time of our Savior, were the custodians of the Scriptures, which they read and explained in the synagogues, and thus were instrumental in keeping alive, however faintly, a knowledge of the true God; so that, with all their defects, this tribe was of signal service to the nation. By the wise separation of this tribe to God, the light of true religion was kept burning amidst surrounding darkness; the ritual services of the tabernacle and temple were attended to; and at least a remnant was always found, even in the worst times, to worship God in the beauty of holiness, and to magnify and declare His great name.

God has, in the Gospel dispensation, made provision for making known His will, instructing His people, and wafting the glad tidings of Salvation— not to one nation only, but to all nations, and peoples, and tongues. He had not seen meet, however, under this, as under the old economy, to choose a particular tribe as His ministering servants in accomplishing these great ends; for while He had given pastors to His church, He had also appointed all believers New Testament Levites, and separated them from the rest of the world unto Himself. He calls upon them all to dedicate themselves to His service.

Now the family heads of the Levites approached Eleazar the priest, Joshua son of Nun, and the heads of the other tribal families of Israel at Shiloh in Canaan and said to them, "The LORD commanded through Moses that you give us towns to live in, with pasturelands for our livestock." So, as the LORD had commanded, the Israelites gave the Levites the following towns and pasturelands out of their own inheritance . . . (Josh. 21:1–3).

I give to the Levites all the tithes in Israel as their inheritance in return for the work they do while serving at the Tent of Meeting (Num. 18:21).

The Levites, when not on duty at the sanctuary, were scattered up and down the whole land, and thus became centers of light from which religious knowledge was diffused. Christ's followers, however, are scattered through all lands, shining as lights in the world, and by the grace of God hastening on the bright era of the millennium glory, when all people shall walk in the light of the Lord and rejoice in Him.

> The beam that shines from Zion Hill
> Shall lighten every land.

If you have believed in Jesus, and would remain His disciple, you cannot escape His service. He claims you as really as He did the first-born Israelites, nay, He has stronger claims on you than He had on them. He spared them from the stroke of the angel of death, but He died on the cross that you might live for ever. Do you, then, feel the paramount claims He has upon you? Do you court rather than shun His service? And are you often asking, "Lord, what wouldst thou have me to do?" If so, then you are doubtless already in harness and aiding on the great work of building up the New Testament church. Work on, whether in instructing little ones in the Sabbath-school, as missionary collectors, as tract distributors, or in any other way God in His providence has opened up for you. God speed your efforts to advance the kingdom of His dear Son. Work on, ever looking upwards to your heavenly Father, and, as your look, exclaiming, "My sufficiency is of Thee," and He will bless you and your work, and receive you to Himself at last with the joyful welcome, "Well done, good and faithful servant; thou hast been faithful over a few things, I will make thee ruler over many things; enter thou into the joy of thy Lord." Never forget your high calling. Wherever you are, at home or abroad, in the midst of saints or sinners, in all places and at all times, seek to adorn the doctrine of God our Savior by a walk and a conversation becoming the gospel. The Levites, remember, were centers of light. You are also called upon to "Let your light shine." "Arise, shine." "Shine ye as lights in the world."

19
THE SACRIFICES UNDER THE LAW

The burnt offering, peace offering, sin offering, and trespass offering were bloody sacrifices, involving the slaying of oxen, sheep, goats, doves, and pigeons. The meat offerings were bloodless oblations, consisting of vegetable productions, such as corn, flour, meal, bread, cakes, oils, and salt. It was not, however, till the Israelites were settled in Canaan, that the whole Levitical law was binding on them or could possibly be obeyed.

The Burnt Offering

The burnt offering was so called because, unlike all other forms of sacrifice, the whole of the body of the victims (the skin only excepted) was entirely consumed by the altar fire, and ascended in smoke to God. Only male animals were permitted to be offered as burnt sacrifices, it was however in the option of the offerer to bring any of the animals already named (Lev. 1), according as his piety might prompt him, or his means might admit of.

When an Israelite brought a bullock as his offering, he led it up to the tabernacle door, where the priests, arrayed in their robes of office, were in attendance; and if on examination they declared it to be without blemish, that is, free from any of the disqualifying defects enumerated in Lev. 22:17–26, he was permitted to offer it to the Lord there, even before the entrance to the holy habitation. Death was the penalty for offering sacrifices elsewhere. This was in order to prevent idolatry. After putting his hand on the head of the victim, and by that solemn act devoting it to the Lord as his substitute or representative, he slew it, probably on the north side of the altar (Lev. 1:11), the officiating priest receiving the blood, and sprinkling it around the under part of the altar. The sacrificer then skinned and cut up the carcass, in which duty he may have been assisted by Levites. The legs and inward were washed with water and sprinkled with salt, and all the parts of the body (some say in nearly their natural order) were laid on the altar by the priest, and the whole being consumed by the fire, ascended in smoke to God, to whom it was of a sweet savor. The sprinkling of blood, and the laying of the parts of the victim on the altar, principally constituted the presenting of the sacrifice.

He is to slaughter it at the north side of the altar before the LORD, *and Aaron's sons the priests shall sprinkle its blood against the altar on all sides (Lev. 1:11).*

A male sheep or goat brought as a burnt offering by an Israelite who may not have been able to afford a bullock, would be as acceptable as the latter, and was presented in the same manner, and with the like ceremonies. It is expressly said that the sheep or goat was slain on the north side of the altar.

A turtle dove, or young pigeon, brought by a poor man, was as efficacious as the offering of his richer neighbor; so that the rich and the poor met on a level at the altar. The priest, not the offerer, killed and prepared the bird for the altar. This, probably, was with a view to save the blood, to effect which great care and much practice were necessary.

The burnt offering was evidently intended to be an expiatory sacrifice—the victim bleeding, suffering, and dying for the sin of the offerer, in order that he might escape deserved punishment; "it was to make an atonement for him." It was a self-dedicatory offering as well, and some are of opinion that self-dedication was pre-eminently its design—the entire body of the victim consumed on the altar being significant of the dedication of the offerer of himself to God. The reference in Rom. 12:1, is evidently to the burnt offering, and helps to confirm this view. The sin offerings and trespass offerings, on the other hand, were pre-eminently expiatory sacrifices. When several offerings were presented to God on the same occasion, the sin

Therefore, I urge you, brothers, in view of God's mercy, to offer your bodies as living sacrifices, holy and pleasing to God—this is your spiritual act of worship (Rom. 12:1).

offering always took precedence—thus seeming to teach, that the offerers were first reconciled to God by the expiatory sacrifice (the sin offering), before, by the burnt offering, they signified the dedication of themselves to Him (Lev. 8:14–16; 9:8–12; 16:1–34). It is also worthy of notice that the first sacrifice offered on the altar was a sin offering. The following are a few of many passages seeming to teach that sin and sins were more intimately associated with sin offerings, than with burnt offerings (compare Lev. 1 with Lev. 4, 5, 6: see Psalm 40:6; Heb. 5:1; 10:6; Lev. 8:14–16; 9:8–12; 16:11–25).

Every high priest is selected from among men and is appointed to represent them in matters related to God, to offer gifts and sacrifices for sins (Heb. 5:1).

Besides free-will burnt offerings, brought as individuals might be prompted, burnt offerings had to be offered by individuals at the removal of ceremonial uncleanness of different kinds (Lev. 12:6; 14:19). The following were the public burnt offerings: daily (Exod. 29:38); weekly (Num. 28:9, 10); monthly (vv. 11–16); yearly (vv. 16–26).

The burnt offering as well as all the other animal sacrifices typified the atoning death of Christ; indeed, apart from His death, that of the various victims slain at the altar had no meaning. The self-dedicatory character of this offering was strikingly fulfilled in the life of Christ. His every word and act while on earth showed how entirely He was devoted to the will of His Father. "Not as I will, but as Thou wilt." "My meat is to do the will of Him that sent me." "Wist ye not that I must be about my Father's business?" "I have glorified Thee on the earth; I have finished the work which Thou gavest Me to do." These were memorable utterances of Him whose life from the manger to the cross was one continual burnt offering.

When the days of her purification for a son or daughter are over, she is to bring to the priest at the entrance to the Tent of Meeting a year-old lamb for a burnt offering and a young pigeon or a dove for a sin offering (Lev. 12:6).

Christians can in no sense fulfill the expiatory aspect of the burnt sacrifice. He who trod the "wine-press alone," has done this once for all by His atoning death. Their duty is to be constantly looking by faith to Him as crucified for them, and to be continually striving, in their daily life, to fulfill the self-dedicatory aspect of the offering. "Ye are bought with a price, therefore glorify God in your body and in your spirit, which are God's." "I beseech you therefore, brethren, by the mercies of God, that ye present your bodies a living sacrifice, holy, acceptable unto God, which is your reasonable service."

The Meat Offering

When the Scriptures were translated into English, "meat" did not mean "flesh," as it does now; it meant food in general. The following were varieties of meat offerings:—*First*, A meat offering of flour, upon which oil has been poured. *Second*, A meat offering baked in the oven, consisting of unleavened cakes of fine flour mingled with oil, or unleavened wafers anointed with oil. *Third*, A meat offering of fine flour unleavened, mingled with oil, and baked in a pan. When baked it was parted in pieces, and oil poured on it, the oil being used as butter is with us on bread. *Fourth*, A meat offering made of fine flour, with oil, and baked in the frying-pan. *Fifth*, A meat offering of first fruits—"green ears of corn dried by the fire," with oil and frankincense (Lev. 2).

When someone brings a grain offering to the LORD, his offering is to be of fine flour. He is to pour oil on it, put incense on it (Lev. 2:1).

The offerer brought his offering—one or other of the foregoing—to the priest, who took a part of it, called a "memorial," which he laid on the altar to be burned. What remained of the offerings, after the memorial or the Lord's part was taken out of them, belonged to the priest. No honey or leaven was allowed to be mixed with the meat offerings (v. 11), but salt (v. 13) was applied to them all. Leaven, though useful in making bread, has a tendency to corruption. Leavened bread will only keep a few days at most, while unleavened bread will keep a long time. This, probably, was the reason that leaven was forbidden in the offerings. Salt has quite an opposite tendency; it is a powerful preservative, and as applied to the offerings, was designed to show the enduring nature of the covenant between God and the Hebrews. Drink offerings of wine commonly accompanied meat offerings. They were, however, never offered separately; and both formed part of the stated public sacrifices offered daily, weekly, monthly, and yearly (Num. 28).

Give this command to the Israelites and say to them: "See that you present to me at the appointed time the food for my offerings made by fire, as an aroma pleasing to me" (Num. 28:2).

By bringing a meat offering, an Israelite dedicated to God a part of the choicest of those temporal

If someone's offering is a fellowship offering, and he offers an animal from the herd, whether male or female, he is to present before the LORD an animal without defect (Lev. 3:1).

mercies constituting his daily bread, and by this act acknowledged that he was indebted to his Maker not only for that sample of His bounties, but for the stock, even for all that he possessed.

Although God did not stand in need of food, yet these gifts were of a sweet savor to Him, and His ministering servants were nourished by them—the greater portion going to them, it being only a small part (the "memorial" or God's part) that was burned on the altar.

Christians should evince their gratitude to God for daily mercies, by bringing gifts and laying them on the New Testament altar. "To do good and to communicate forget not; for with such sacrifices God is well pleased."

Peace Offering

The priest shall burn the fat on the altar, but the breast belongs to Aaron and his sons. You are to give the right thigh of your fellowship offerings to the priest as a contribution (Lev. 7:31–32).

Peace offerings were taken from the herd or from the flock, and consisted of the same kind of animals that formed the burnt offerings, and, like them, required to be without blemish; they might, however, either be male or female (Lev. 3). They were slain and skinned, and their blood sprinkled in the same manner as the burnt offerings, but only the fatty parts were burned. The priests got the breast and the right shoulder (Lev. 7:31–34), which, from the peculiar way they had to present these to the Lord, the one being lifted or heaved up and down, and the other waved to and fro from right to left in the air (vv. 30, 32), were called the "heave" and "wave" offerings. All that remained of the carcass belonged to the offerer, who might invite his friends and the poor to feast on it along with him. The priests ate their own portion, and the altar fire devoured God's part. The offering being thus shared among these three parties, and each of them partaking of it, signified their being at peace and holding communion together, hence the offering is appropriately call a peace offering. Peace offerings of a national character, and on a grand scale, were sometimes offered (Lev. 9:18; Josh. 8:31; 2 Sam. 6:17; 1 Kings 8:62, etc.).

He slaughtered the ox and the ram as the fellowship offering for the people. His sons handed him the blood, and he sprinkled it against the altar on all sides (Lev. 9:18).

Although this offering had an expiatory character, its main design does not appear to have been to make atonement for sins, nor to represent the self-dedication of the offerer to God, but rather to express thankfulness to God. Hence it is sometimes called a "thank offering." An Israelite wishing to express thankfulness to God for mercies received, might do so by bringing a peace offering; or, if he wished to supplicate for blessings, he brought the same form of offerings, thus thanking God for past, while soliciting new favors. Peace offerings were evidently intended to keep alive in the bosoms of the Israelites the combined flame of gratitude, piety, and charity.

If the anointed priest sins, bringing guilt on the people, he must bring to the LORD a young bull without defect as a sin offering for the sin he has committed (Lev. 4:3).

The Sin Offering and the Trespass Offering

The "burnt offering" represented chiefly the dedication to God of a portion of the good things with which the offerer had been favored by providence; the "peace offering" was expressive of the offerer's gratitude to God for mercies received, or of his desire or prayer for new ones. The "burnt offering" and the "peace offering" had also, as we have seen, an expiatory character, but this does not seem to have been their main feature. The main idea, however, of the "sin offering" and the "trespass offering" was that of expiation. These sacrifices were offered for the expiation of certain specified sins (Lev. 4, 5, 6).

The Sin Offering

The animals used for sin offerings, with the exception of birds, were the same as those for burnt offerings. The particular one, however, the offerer was required to bring was prescribed by law, yet with an obvious regard to his position in the commonwealth (Lev. 4:3–28).

When a leader sins unintentionally and does what is forbidden in any of the commands of the LORD his God, he is guilty. When he is made aware of the sin he committed, he must bring as his offering a male goat without defect (Lev. 4:22–23).

The priest's offering.—A priest who had committed any of the specified sins, brought a young bullock, without blemish (Lev. 4:3–13), to the door of the tabernacle, and there, putting his hands on its head, confessed audibly (according to Jewish writers) the sin he was guilty of, and for which he desired it to make atonement. Having slain it, he carried its blood into the holy place, and there sprinkled the blood seven times before the veil of the sanctuary, rubbed

If the whole Israelite community sins unintentionally and does what is forbidden in any of the LORD's commands, even though the community is unaware of the matter, they are guilty. When they become aware of the sin they committed, the assembly must bring a young bull as a sin offering and present it before the Tent of Meeting (Lev. 4:13–14).

some of it on each of the horns of the golden altar, and on returning to the court, poured out the residue at the foot of the brazen altar. After this, he took off from the carcass the fatty parts, and put them on the altar, where they were burned, and ascended in smoke to God. The fatty parts, next to the blood of the animal, were considered the most precious. All that remained (the head, the flesh, the legs, and the dung) he was required to carry (of course, with the assistance of the Levites) out of the court, and beyond the camp, to a clean place, where the ashes from the altar were poured out, and there burn them.

The sin offering for the congregation.—The sin offering for the whole congregation was the same as that for the priest—a young bullock without blemish (Lev. 4:13–22). It was brought by the representatives of the congregation, the elders, who put their hands on its head, confessing, as they did so, the particular sins of which the people had been guilty. It was slain either by the elders or the priest. The ceremony of sprinkling the blood, burning the fatty parts on the altar, and removing the remainder of the carcass beyond the camp, was the same as in the case of the priest's offering.

The ruler's sin offering.—The ruler's offering was a young he-goat (Lev. 4:22–27). Having put his hands on its head, and confessed his sins over it, he slew it. The priest having received the blood, dipped his finger in it, and rubbed it on the horns of the altar of burnt offerings, and then poured out what was left at the foot of the altar. After this, he burned the fatty parts of the animal on the altar fire. What remained of the victim was not carried beyond the camp, as was the case with the priests' and the congregation's offering, but became the property of the priests, who feasted upon it in the holy place.

If a member of the community sins unintentionally and does what is forbidden in any of the LORD's commands, he is guilty. When he is made aware of the sin he committed, he must bring as his offering for the sin he committed a female goat without defect (Lev. 4:27–28).

The common person's offering.—If one of the common people had sinned, the law prescribed for his offering either a young she-goat or a she-lamb (Lev. 4:27–35). It was presented to God in the same way, and with the like ceremony as the ruler's offering.

The sprinkling of the blood before the veil, and the carrying of the carcass beyond the camp to be burned, in the cases of the priests' and congregation's offerings, were intended to denote that the sins of the priests were more heinous than the same sins committed by a private Israelite; and that the sins of a whole congregation were more heinous than the same sins when committed by a single individual.

The Trespass Offering

It is not easy to distinguish, in some cases, between the sins and offenses for which the law prescribed a "trespass offering" or a "sin offering" but you will find the particular sins for both classes of sacrifices enumerated in Lev. 4, 5, and 6. "Sin offerings," we have seen, might be brought by priest, congregation, ruler, or private person; trespass offerings, however, were only to be brought by individuals (Lev. 5:1–19). The usual animal for a trespass offering was a young she-goat or she-lamb; but a poor person was permitted to bring two turtle doves or two young pigeons—the one to be offered as a trespass offering, and the other as a burnt offering; or if he were too poor to offer these, the law mercifully admitted of his bringing instead a meat offering of fine flour, which, however, was not regarded as a meat offering, but as a trespass offering, and hence had an expiatory character which the ordinary meat offering had not. Although a she-lamb or she-goat was the usual trespass offering, yet some trespasses, looked upon as peculiarly heinous, such as those "in the holy things of the Lord," required the sacrificer to bring a ram.

The sacrifices under the law effected the temporal remission of punishment, they could not, however, cleanse the soul from the guilt of sin, nor purchase spiritual and eternal blessings; for "it is not possible that the blood of bulls and of goats should take away sins" (Heb. 10:4; 9:12–16). An Israelite who, by sinning, had incurred the penalty of death, provided he had not sinned presumptuously (that is, knowingly, willfully, and deliberately), on bringing the prescribed offering, was pardoned (Lev. 4:20, 26, 31, 35; Num. 15:28, etc.); or, one who had become unclean either by violations of the ceremonial law or otherwise,

. . . and, as a penalty for the sin he has committed, he must bring to the LORD a female lamb or goat from the flock as a sin offering; and the priest shall make atonement for him for his sin (Lev. 5:6).

He did not enter by means of the blood of goats and calves; but he entered the Most Holy Place once for all by his own blood, having obtained eternal redemption (Heb. 9:12).

and, in consequence, had been banished from the encampment, on bringing the prescribed sacrifice, was cleansed, and restored to his place in the congregation (Lev. 13:46–59; 14, 15; Num. 12:15). And, in general, to the individual or nation sacrificing, as the case might be, were continued those distinguished temporal blessings and privileges which as a people the Hebrews enjoyed. To what extent the bulk of the nation understood the typical import of the sacrifices we are not informed; it cannot, however, be doubted that these sacrifices were means of grace to pious Israelites, who were sincerely striving after deliverance, not merely from temporal punishment of sin, but also from its spiritual and eternal penal consequences. Such Israelites had glimpses through these types of the coming Messiah, and by faith in Him as their sin offering to be sacrificed for them had their consciences purged from the guilt of sin by virtue of His atoning blood. Some, no doubt, had stronger faith, and saw with greater clearness than others. Job could say, "I know that my Redeemer liveth," and the seraphic Isaiah depicted the great sacrifice as distinctly as if with his bodily eyes he had witnessed the crucifixion.

The bloody sacrifices, and especially sin offerings, prefigured the offering of Christ for the sins of men. The animals were innocent, so was He who died, not for His own, but others' sins. Some of them were not only innocent, but patient, meek, and gentle: and He whom they prefigured was meek and lowly. "He is brought as a lamb to the slaughter, and as a sheep before her shearers is dumb, so He openeth not His mouth." The animals were without blemish, and He whom they typified was "without spot," "holy, harmless, undefiled, and separate from sinners." The eyes, not of erring priests, but those of the all-seeing Jehovah, search the great Victim, and find no fault in Him; "This is my beloved Son, in whom I am well pleased." The offerer put his hands on the head of the devoted animal, symbolically transferring his guilt to it. On Jesus hath been laid "the iniquity of us all." The animals were slain. He is the Lamb of God "slain from the foundation of the world." They bled. Behold the blood flowing from the pierced side of the Redeemer. The sprinkling of the blood was the most solemn act of the priestly office. So Christ's blood shed, signifies his life given for sinners; "Who gave Himself a ransom for all." His blood sprinkled on a sinner's conscience saves from spiritual and eternal death. What of the victim's body was burned on the altar prefigured the sufferings of Him who groaned and bled on Calvary's cross. The carcass of the animal, in the cases of the priests' and the congregation's offerings, being burned beyond the camp, denoted the heinousness of sin when committed by those parties; and so Christ was crucified not within but beyond the walls of Jerusalem ("without the gate," Heb. 13:12); thus signifying that the sins for which He suffered were of the deepest dye, and those not of a nation merely, but of people of every nation; for "He is the propitiation for our sins; and not for ours only, but also for the sins of the whole world: (1 John 2:2). If an Israelite transgressed the law, he could escape the punishment of his sin (if it were death) by no other means than by sacrifice; or, having contracted ceremonial uncleanness, could not be restored to his place in the congregation, nor be allowed to visit the courts of God's house, unless he brought the prescribed bloody offering. "Without shedding of blood is no remission." This speaks to us with no uncertain sound of the "great sacrifice," and of His precious blood as that alone which can give peace to a troubled conscience, save sinners from spiritual and eternal death, and gain admission for them at last into the courts of the heavenly temple. Blessed by God, "the blood of Jesus Christ His Son cleanseth us from all sin."

And so Jesus also suffered outside the city gate to make the people holy through his own blood (Heb. 13:12).

Have you peace with God through our Lord Jesus Christ? If not, remember there is salvation in no other. If you continue to reject Him, your iniquity must remain for ever on your own head, and you will never be able to escape from an avenging God, nor from an accusing conscience, nor from the pains of hell. Escape for your life from so terrible a doom. "For if the word spoken by angels was steadfast, and every transgression and disobedience received a just recompense of reward; how shall we escape if we neglect so great salvation." Escape now; tomorrow may be too late. The gate of the court with the beautiful inscription, "The Door of Mercy" inscribed on its portals, is still open, and if you bend your ear you will hear the sweet voice of Him who is priest, sacrifice, and altar all in one, inviting you to enter and approach, in these winsome words: "Him that cometh unto Me, I will in no wise cast out." Do enter, we entreat you; and drawing near to Him and putting your hands on his devoted head, say—

> I lay my sins on Jesus,
>   The spotless Lamb of God;
> He bears them all and frees us
>   From the accursed load.
> I bring my guilt to Jesus,
>   To wash my crimson stains
> White in His blood most precious
>   Till not a spot remains.

20
THE DAILY SERVICE

The priests began their morning duties by removing (with whatever help was necessary from their assistants, the Levites) the ashes accumulated in consequence of the burnt offering of the previous evening, to the place appointed for them beyond the camp (Lev. 6:10, 11), and by supplying the fire with fresh fuel. After this, having washed at the laver, and put on their official robes—the garments for glory and for beauty—they were ready to begin the work of daily atonement. The altar fire is now blazing, and the curling smoke ascending heavenwards. There stands Aaron resplendent in his golden vestments, the jewels on his breast sparkling in the morning sun, and beside him are his sons attired in raiment pure and white. The worshippers who are now entering the court are the national representatives (the elders). At length a lamb is led to the door of the tabernacle, where it is carefully examined by the priests; and, being a male of the first year, and without spot or defect, is declared to be a proper victim, and is then led to the north side of the altar, where it is slain, and its body burned in the same manner as the private offerings already described. A meat offering of flour mingled with oil, and a drink offering of wine, accompany the burnt offering (Exod. 29:38–46).

The other principal part of the morning service was the offering of incense. The high priest, or other priest appointed to this duty, entered the holy place in the morning. His first business was with the golden candlestick. He trimmed the lamps one by one,

The priest shall then put on his linen clothes, with linen undergarments next to his body, and shall remove the ashes of the burnt offering that the fire has consumed on the altar and place them beside the altar. Then he is to take off these clothes and put on others, and carry the ashes outside the camp to a place that is ceremonially clean (Lev. 6:10–11).

This is what you are to offer on the altar regularly each day: two lambs a year old (Exod. 29:38).

Do not offer on this altar any other incense or any burnt offering or grain offering, and do not pour a drink offering on it (Exod. 30:9).

removing any dust or other defilement that may have gathered on it during the night, so that it might stand pure and spotless. The lamps, furnished with fresh oil, burned brilliantly, affording ample light to enable the priests to officiate in the sanctuary. Repairing now to the court, he filled a censer with fire from off the brazen altar; and, re-entering the holy place, put it on the golden altar, at the same time dropping a handful of incense on the fire. Immediately clouds pregnant with sweet odors arose, and, penetrating through the veil, were borne onward to Israel's God enthroned in visible symbol on the mercy seat (Exod. 30:7–11).

No mention is made of sacred song in connection with the tabernacle worship in the wilderness; but in the holy land it formed part of the sacred service, no fewer than four thousand Levites being specially set apart by David for conducting the praises of God's house.

The service in the evening was nearly similar to that of the morning.

By means of the morning and evening services, the respective sins of the past night and day were atoned for, thus securing at least the remission of temporal punishment, and the continuance of God's gracious presence in the midst of Israel.

The devotion of the whole animal, as a sacrifice, was representative of the people anew dedicating themselves wholly to God. The meat offering accompanying the sacrifice of the morning and evening lamb was an acknowledgment of God as the bestower of daily mercies. While thanking God by it for mercies received, they also by it looked to Him as the source from whence fresh supplies were to be drawn, so that through this offering we may hear the voice of supplication, as well as of thanksgiving, saying "Give us this day our daily bread." How meet it was that the Israelites, favored by God above all the nations of the earth, should begin and end the day with these appropriate services! By the offering of incense the priest symbolically interceded with God for the people, the ascending perfumed cloud being the nation's embodied prayer. Israelites in the court, and not improbably many who gathered around the sacred precincts without, as well as the pious throughout the camp, knowing the time of incense (Luke 1:10), made it a time of prayer; so that with the morning and evening incense, their united supplications might blend, and together reach the mercy seat.

The two chief parts of the morning and evening service were typical of the two great parts of Christ's work. The lamb sacrificed typified His atonement, and the offering of incense His intercession. The daily burnt offering, more significantly than the free-will burnt offerings, prefigured the death of Christ; for while these might be taken from oxen, sheep, goats, or doves, that must be a lamb. Christ is never called an ox, a sheep, or a goat, but He is named the "Lamb of God." It also foreshadowed more significantly than these other sacrifices the necessity of daily application of the blood of Jesus to a sinner's conscience, in order to procure his forgiveness. The offering of incense prefigures the intercession of Him, who, with His own blood, passed through the veil into the true Holy of Holies; where, at the heavenly throne, He ever liveth to plead its merits, on behalf of His believing people, as He presents their evening and morning prayers, as well as all their holy breathings to His and their heavenly Father.

And when the time for the burning of incense came, all the assembled worshipers were praying outside (Luke 1:10).

In the more corrupt ages of Jewish history, the offering of sacrifices and of incense became a dead letter, to the great majority of both priests and people. For by engaging in the services of the sanctuary with impure and impenitent hearts, the people let their sacrifices and their incense become an "abomination to Him" (Prov. 15:8; Isa. 1:10–17). This sad result, however, did not arise from any defect in these means of grace. They were God's appointed means for the spiritual growth of His ancient people, and it was in a prayerful improvement of them that Old Testament saints were made meet for the inheritance of the saints in light. Daily communion with God tended to keep the flame of spiritual life alive in their souls. God's promise to those who frequented the sanctuary was "There I will meet with thee." The language of

The LORD detests the sacrifice of the wicked, but the prayer of the upright pleases him (Prov. 15:8).

pious souls was, "We shall be satisfied with the goodness of Thy house, even of Thy holy temple;" and,
when deprived of the privilege of worshipping there,
they ardently longed for a renewal of it—

> My thirsty soul longs veh'mently,
>   Yea faints, Thy courts to see;
> My very heart and flesh cry out,
>   O living God for Thee.

There were always some, even in the most corrupt
ages of Jewish history, who worshipped God in spirit
and in truth, and who, like David and Isaiah, and
Zacharias the priest, and good old Simeon, drew
water daily out of these wells of salvation, and in
every bleeding sacrifice beheld the bleeding "lamb of
God." It is so still. The means of grace to some are a
savor of life, to others a savor of death. There are still,
as of old, many merely formal worshippers. On the
other hand, there are many, and an ever-increasing
number, who profit by waiting upon the Lord in the
Christian assembly, and delight greatly when their
steps are bent thitherward, like the pious worshipper
of old who sang joyfully, "I was glad when they said
unto me, Let us go into the house of the Lord."

Your New Moon festivals
and your appointed
feasts
my soul hates.
They have become a
burden to me;
I am weary of bearing
them (Isa. 1:14).

And while in the sanctuary they engage in spirit
in the same exercises as Old Testament saints did in
the tabernacle and temple, the great sacrifice is held
up in the Christian assembly, not in type but in truth.
Every faithful minister of the gospel considers it his
greatest honor and privilege to hold it up. "God forbid
that I should glory save in the cross of our Lord Jesus
Christ." There, too, incense is offered up—even the
praise and prayers that ascend from the altar of
renewed hearts—to the heavenly throne. Do you
delight in visiting the courts of the Lord's house? If
so, it is well. Wait upon the Lord there, and you shall
be satisfied with the goodness of God's house, even of
His holy temple. Few sanctuaries are open for worship
on the ordinary days of the week; but we believe the
time is coming, and may be near at hand, when in
every town or district, at least the doors of one
Christian meeting-place will be thrown open for

those who are inclined, and who can find it convenient to come together to seek God's face, and communion with Him who has said, "Where two or three are gathered together in My name, there am I in the midst." The privilege of daily worship may be enjoyed at the family altar, and by all believers in their own closets, and surely no true Christian will be content with less than morning and evening service. Christians are under deeper obligations than Old Testament saints were, to begin and end the day with exercises implying thankfulness for mercies received, sorrow for sin, the consecration of themselves, and all they have, to Him who bought them with His own precious blood. Our first look every morning, and our last one every night, should be to the atoning Lamb of God; our first notes of praise when we awake, and our last ones ere we fall asleep, should be songs of praise to our adorable Redeemer; our first givings at the dawn of day, and our last at its close, should be the giving of ourselves anew to Him who gave Himself for us. If we live in daily communion with God, we will go on unto perfection, every day exhibiting more and more of the beauty of holiness. Thus living, we need not be afraid to die. How calmly at night we may lay our head on our pillow, and close our eyes, knowing if they should never open again here, they will open in that bright world where there is no night, but endless day; or, when leaving our dwellings in the morning to pursue our daily calling, how cheerfully we may go forth, knowing that if death should overtake us by the way, and prevent us from ever again re-entering our earthly habitation, we shall find a home in the skies. Or should we, like the great majority of our fellows, have some little warning of our approaching desolation, how peaceful our dying-bed will be: the entrance of the last enemy into our chamber will not overwhelm us with terror. Having long been in the daily habit of looking with child-like trust to Jesus, and of committing our souls to His keeping, we know that He will not forsake us when we come to stand on Jordan's bank, but will fulfill His promise, "When thou passest through the waters, I will be with thee." He will then hold out to us His own loving and almighty hand; and as we place ours in it for the last time on this side of the river, we need not fear, but feel safe and happy, assured that He will conduct us in safety through the stream—"The narrow stream of death"—and bring us into the better land, and into His Father's house of many mansions.

> Jesus, the vision of Thy face
>   Hath overpowering charms,
> Scarce shall I feel death's cold embrace,
>   If Christ be in my arms.

21
THE GREAT DAY OF ATONEMENT

A great day in Israel was the tenth of the seventh month (our September). The people, who were early astir, might have been seen in multitudes crowding to the sanctuary, in obedience to the divine command, "Ye shall have on this day an holy convocation" (Num. 29:7). All secular work was suspended: "It shall be a Sabbath of rest" (lit. Sabbath of Sabbaths) "unto you" (Lev. 16:31). It was also a day of humiliation on account of the sins of the past year: "Ye shall afflict your souls" (v. 29). National sin not only polluted the people, but also the beautiful sanctuary, and so defiled them and it as to render it necessary, in addition to all the sacrifices offered during the preceding twelve months, that they and it should this day be purged with atoning blood.

On the tenth day of this seventh month hold a sacred assembly. You must deny yourselves and do no work (Num. 29:7).

Offerings Peculiar to This Day

Besides the usual stated daily burnt offering, there was an additional one this day, consisting of one young bullock, one ram, and seven lambs, with the accompanying meat and drink offerings (Num. 29:7, 8). The special offerings, however (Lev. 16), were:—

Present as an aroma pleasing to the LORD a burnt offering of one young bull, one ram and seven male lambs a year old, all without defect (Num. 29:8).

First, A young bullock for a sin offering for Aaron and his house.

Second, Two goats for a sin offering for the people.

Third, A ram for a burnt offering for Aaron and his house.

Fourth, A ram for a burnt offering for the people.

Much is said about the sin offerings in Lev. 16; little, however, about the other forms of sacrifice, and this is quite in keeping with the character of the day of atonement, for the former in a much higher degree than the latter had an expiatory character.

High Priest Officiating in White Robes

Aaron having washed his whole body in water, and dressed (v. 4), not in the high priest's colored robes, but simply in the white linen garments, began the services peculiar to the day of annual atonement by presenting at the door of the tabernacle the bullock for himself and his house, and then the two goats for the people, upon which he cast lots—one lot for the Lord, and the other lot for the scapegoat. The goat upon which the lot fell for the Lord he again presented before the Lord at the door of the tabernacle. The first time it, along with the other, formed one united offering; the second time it was for a sin offering to be sacrificed in the usual way. This, however, was not to be the destiny of its fellow, for when again presented, it was as a live goat to be sent away alive as the scapegoat into the wilderness.

High Priest in the Holy of Holies

Aaron, after slaying the bullock for himself and his house, entered the tabernacle, carrying in one hand a censer filled with burning coals of fire from off the brazen altar, and in the other sweet incense. The golden candlestick on the left, the shewbread table on the right, and the golden altar before him, were sacred yet familiar objects; but on this peculiarly solemn occasion, he was on his way to the holy of holies, where God in visible symbol was enthroned on the ark of the covenant. For the last twelve months no one, not even the high priest, had visited this innermost chamber of the Holy One of Israel. With the deepest reverence, Aaron lifted the veil, and immediately on entering placed the censer on the ground, dropping at the same time the incense on the fire, so that clouds of sweet odors at once arose and practically hid the shekinah; had this not occurred he might not have dared to look upon the symbol of the Divine presence. Leaving the incense burning, he retraced his steps to the court, and there receiving the blood of the slain bullock, returned to the throne room, and sprinkled it with his finger upon the mercy seat eastward, and before the mercy seat with his finger seven times. The blood he sprinkled was an acknowledgment that, on account of the sins of the past year, he and his house were unclean and deserved death; but on the ground of that blood, cried for and obtained forgiveness and cleansing.

The goat upon which the lot fell for the Lord, being the people's sin offering, was now slain by Aaron, who, carrying its blood into the holy of holies, sprinkled it in the same manner as he had done that of the bullock; and as for himself in his previous entry, so now for them he asks and obtains forgiveness of the sins they had been guilty of during the past year. His reappearance in the court is the signal that all Israel is pardoned.

Once a year Aaron shall make atonement on its horns. This annual atonement must be made with the blood of the atoning sin offering for the generations to come. It is most holy to the LORD (Exod. 30:10).

The Tabernacle Cleansed

The tabernacle as well as the people required cleansing, for it was polluted by reason of the sins of those in whose midst it stood. The sprinkling of the blood upon the mercy seat and before the mercy seat has sufficed for the cleansing of the most holy place, as well as for Aaron and the people. The holy place must likewise be cleansed. With the mingled blood of both sin-offerings, Aaron, approaching the golden altar (Lev. 16:18; Exod. 30:10), rubbed the blood seven times; by this rite both the altar and the holy place were cleansed. The remainder of the blood was poured out at the foot of the brazen altar, constituting its cleansing and that of the court in which it stood, for almost all things are by the law purged with blood.

For Aaron, his house, the people, the holy of holies, the incense-altar, and the holy place, the altar of burnt offerings and the court, atonement has now been made—all these have been cleansed with blood.

The people did not fear now that, on account of the sins of the past year, flashes of fire from the cloudy pillar would consume them, nor the plague destroy them, nor their Divine King depart from their midst. He will continue to dwell in the beautiful tabernacle as His palace temple, and suffer the people to approach and hold communion with Him through the medium of the high priest.

The Scapegoat

After such significant rites, all pointing to the remission of sin and to the complete cleansing of the people, was anything further done on this great day in order to set forth the complete blotting out of sin? Yes, behold the scapegoat!

On the great day of atonement, two goats formed one combined offering for the people. One was slain, and as we have already seen, its blood sprinkled on the mercy seat, in virtue of which the national sins of the past year were forgiven. The sins already atoned for were now put (symbolically) upon the head of the live or scapegoat, in order to give the Israelites a more vivid sense of how graciously and completely God had forgiven their sins. So laden, the goat was led by a fit man into the wilderness. This man led the goat down the court, out at the gate, through the streets formed by the tents of the thousands of Israel, and when beyond the encampment, into the wilderness, where it was lost. There it may

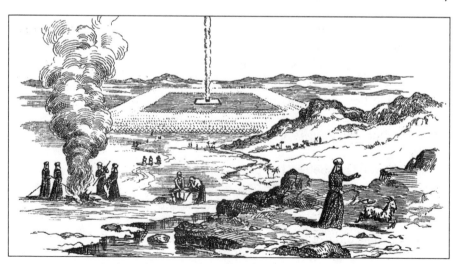

Fire beyond camp.   Great Day of Atonement.   Scapegoat.

have been torn to pieces by wild beasts, or may have died a slow agonizing death from hunger and thirst, or from some other cause. We are not told how or when it died, and it is not necessary we should be, for it was not its final doom that was intended to be portrayed in vivid color to the Israelites, but the great and comforting truth, that God this day had so completely forgiven His people, as to look upon them in their relation to Him as King of Israel as if they had never sinned at all. The sins that the goat bore away into the wilderness were for ever lost, so that they should never be remembered against the congregation. Their sins were removed to such a distance from Him that when "sought for they shall not be found." The people did not see the blood sprinkled on the mercy seat; in the scapegoat, however, burdened with the nation's sins, being sent away into the wilderness, they had a visible and striking symbol set before their wondering eyes of the complete forgiveness of their sins as a nation, by God. Their sins were for ever removed out of His sight.

He is to cast lots for the two goats—one lot for the LORD and the other for the scapegoat. Aaron shall bring the goat whose lot falls to the LORD and sacrifice it for a sin offering. But the goat chosen by lot as the scapegoat shall be presented alive before the LORD to be used for making atonement by sending it into the desert as a scapegoat (Lev. 16:8–10).

Thus God for Christ's sake completely forgives the sins of believers. He acts as if He both forgave and forgot. When the believer looks up into the smiling face of his Heavenly Father, he will never see there the slightest trace of the remembrance of past and forgiven sins flitting across the divine countenance; "as far as the east is from the west, so far hath He removed our transgressions from us."

The Two Goats—Two Features of the Same Picture

The goat that was sacrificed and the one that was sent into the wilderness are two features of the same picture. The blood of the slain goat sprinkled on the mercy seat, signified that pardon and cleansing were obtained through the shed blood of the innocent victim. The sins put upon the head of the live goat would have had no significance whatever, had the blood of the slain goat not already been sprinkled upon and before the mercy seat, for "without shedding of blood is no remission." The two goats, in a

He shall bathe himself with water in a holy place and put on his regular garments. Then he shall come out and sacrifice the burnt offering for himself and the burnt offering for the people, to make atonement for himself and for the people (Lev. 16:24).

sense, were one sacrifice, two halves of a whole. If life could have been restored to the dead goat, it would have been dispensed with.

While Aaron was engaged in the solemn work of annual atonement, he was dressed, as we have seen, in white garments only; having slain the sin offerings, and sprinkled their blood, as already described, he entered the holy place, and again washed his body in water (Lev. 16:24), and arrayed himself in the golden robes (Lev. 16:24), so that when he reappeared in the court he was resplendent in his shining and colored vestments.

By the atonement made this day for Israel, the barriers standing in the way of their approach to God were removed, so that they might now approach Him through the medium of the high priest. The way of access being open, Aaron now offered the burnt offerings; the ram for himself, and the ram for the people. After this he burned the fat of his own and the people's sin offering on the altar.

The Altar beyond the Encampment

On the fire without the camp (see illustration, p. 138), the bodies of the animals slain as sin offerings for the high priest and the congregation were consumed, and not in the court altar fire, it being deemed too good or not sufficiently significant for the purpose. A high priest's sins and a nation's sins were considered more heinous in the sight of God than those of private individuals, and consequently a kind of reproach was associated with the bodies of the victims sacrificed for the high priest and for the people. And to emphasize this in a significant manner they were removed out of the court to the fire beyond the camp and burned on it (see illustration, p. 138).

Spiritual Significance

Some aspects of Christ's atoning death were thereby prefigured. Christ died for sins of deepest dye, and He died not for an individual, or for a few persons, not even for a nation. He died for the sins of the world; and hence in keeping with the type, He died not in Jerusalem, but without the walls. "Let us therefore," as we read in Hebrews, "go unto Him without the gate, bearing His reproach." "Without the gate" is equivalent to "without the camp," so that type and antitype agree.

A Laver beyond the Encampment

To impress the people that God was a holy God, and that sin was hateful in His sight, the man who led the goat into the wilderness, as well as the priests and the Levites who carried the bodies of the slain bullock and the goat to the fire without the camp, having thereby become ceremonially unclean, had to wash their hands at a vessel of water beyond the camp ere they returned to the court (see illustration, p. 138).

The Spiritual Significance

of this for us in now apparent. Who may now approach God acceptably and thereby enjoy the light of His countenance? "He that hath clean hands and a pure heart. Holiness becometh Thine house, O Lord, for ever."

There was, as we have seen, an altar and a laver beyond the camp in order to emphasize the solemn truths taught on the great day of annual atonement (see illustration, p. 138).

Christ and the Great Day of Atonement

The whole of the rites of this day were typical of the atoning work of our Great High Priest. Aaron's washing himself and putting on white raiment, and making atonement for his own sins before doing so for the people, shadowed forth the necessity of the perfect holiness of our Great High Priest. He "offered Himself without spot to God."

No one was in the tabernacle when Aaron officiated on the great day of annual atonement, and this circumstance points to Christ's having the sole merit of atonement. He shares it with no one. He trod the wine-press alone.

The high priest, as we have seen, after slaying the sin offerings, carried their blood into the most holy place, and there, amidst clouds of incense covering the golden throne, sprinkled it on the mercy seat, and interceded with God for Israel; the clouds of incense being his embodied prayer, and the sprinkled blood the ground on which forgiveness and all needed blessings were sought. So Christ, our great high priest, after dying for sinners on the cross, ascended up on high, and, parting the blue veil of the skies, entered the true holy of holies, carrying with Him, not the blood of bulls and goats, but His own; and there, where the incense of His all-prevailing intercession not only covers the mercy seat, but fills all heaven with its grateful odors, He ever liveth to plead its merits on behalf of His believing people.

> Once in the circuit of a year,
>   With blood, but not his own,
> Aaron within the veil appears
>   Before the golden throne.

> But Christ, by His own powerful blood,
>   Ascends above the skies,
> And in the presence of our God
>   Shows His own sacrifice.

We have seen what the atonement made on this day effected for the Israelites. As far as pertaineth to the flesh they were cleansed; and their sins, as far at least as they deserved temporal punishment, were forgiven. Spiritual and eternal blessings, however, could only be obtained through the medium of a greater high priest and a greater sin offering—even through Christ. His blood—His alone—can sanctify to the cleansing of a guilty conscience, save from everlasting punishment, and bring sinners near to the Holy One of Israel.

> Not all the blood of beasts,
>   On Jewish altars slain,
> Could give the guilty conscience peace,
>   Or wash away the stain.

> But Christ, the Lamb of God,
>   Takes all our sins away;
> A sacrifice of richer blood
>   And nobler name then they.

Believing, we rejoice
　　To see the curse remove;
We bless the Lamb with cheerful voice,
　　And sing His dying love.

Pious Hebrews, having faith in God and in the appointed means of grace, were partakers, not only of temporal benefits, but also of those spiritual and eternal blessings which Christ, by His atoning death—so vividly prefigured on the day of annual atonement—has secured for the whole household of faith. And we believe that many, if not all, of those who were Israelites indeed, had glimpses, more or less distinct, through the typical services of the great day of atonement of the coming Messiah.

At the conclusion of the services Aaron blessed the congregation: our Great High Priest ever liveth to shower down blessings, great and without number, upon His people.

The day of annual atonement was the greatest day in the Jewish year; great, however, as it was, it was but the shadow of greater days.

The day on which Christ was born in Bethlehem and laid in the manger; the day on which He hung upon Calvary's cross, and which heard His dying accents proclaiming to the ends of the earth, and to the end of time, redemption's completed work, "it is finished;" the day on which He arose triumphant from the grave; and the day on which He ascended from Mount Olivet: these are the greatest days in the world's history, perhaps in that of the universe. They stand out by themselves from all the days of the past, and, with the day of judgment, will do so from all the days of the future.

The grand lesson to be learned from the subject we have been considering is that "without shedding of blood is no remission." May we ever be seeking to have our consciences sprinkled with the precious blood of Christ, and we shall "Have redemption through His blood, even the forgiveness of sins," access at all times to a throne of grace, enjoy the light of God's countenance now, and hereafter dwell for ever in heaven His holy habitation.

When Christ came as high priest of the good things that are already here, he went through the greater and more perfect tabernacle that is not man-made, that is to say, not a part of this creation. He did not enter by means of the blood of goats and calves; but he entered the Most Holy Place once for all by his own blood, having obtained eternal redemption (Heb. 9:11–12).

22
THE SUPERIORITY OF THE HOLY OF HOLIES

We have chosen the above heading for the purpose of hanging on it a few remarks on some points we would not like altogether to pass over. Such points as the variety in value of different parts of the structure and of the holy vessels, the shape of places, the numbers that are prominent in the court and in the tabernacle, and the bearing which these and some other things have on the relative sacredness and importance of the court, the holy place, and the holy of holies.

Make the tabernacle with ten curtains of finely twisted linen and blue, purple and scarlet yarn, with cherubim worked into them by a skilled craftsman (Exod. 26:1).

The superiority of the holy of holies shown by the door pillars.—The gate pillars were overlaid with brass, and stood on brazen sockets; those of the doors of the holy place were superior, for they were overlaid with gold though they stood in brazen sockets; those, however, of the veil or door of the holy of holies were superior to both, not only being overlaid with gold, but having silver sockets to rest on. Thus, the nearer the door pillars approached the holy of holies they increased in beauty and in value.

The superiority of the holy of holies shown by the door hangings.—The hanging for the door or gate of the court was made of blue, and purple, and scarlet, and fine twined linen; that of the door of the holy place, although made of the same material, being four-square, was superior in shape to that of the gate; the veil or door of the holy of holies, however, was superior to both, for besides being four-square and variegated by the same bright colors as the others, it was of cunning work, having cherubim figures interwoven.

Thus, the nearer the door hangings approached the holy of holies they increased in beauty and in richness.

The superiority of the holy of holies as shown by the curtains.—The curtains which with the pillars formed the court wall were made of fine twined linen; those for the holy place were superior, being manufactured of blue, and purple, and scarlet, and fine twined linen, and, with the exception of those for the east side, had figures of cherubim interwoven; those of the holy of holies, as a whole, were superior to those of the holy place, for all its sides—the roof, and the south, north, east, and west walls—shone replendently with the lovely cherubim figures. Thus the nearer the curtains approached the holy of holies they increased in beauty, in richness, and in splendor.

The superiority of the holy of holies shown by the disposition of the coverings and curtains.—Outermost was the covering of badger or sealskins; next, below them the covering of rams' skins dyed red, probably considered finer than the former; next, and below the rams' skins, the fine white silky goat-hair curtains, being finer than the skin coverings; and lastly, and undercoats, and finest of all, and visible in the interior of the house, while the others were not, the splendid cherubim curtains. Thus, the nearer the coverings and curtains came to the interior of the divine dwelling, they increased in fineness, in richness, and in beauty. A striking indication of the cherubim curtains being deemed superior to the goat-hair curtains is the circumstance that, while the two grand divisions of the latter were united by means of loops of blue and clasps of brass, the clasps in the case of the former were of gold. These gold clasps or taches appearing right above and down the sides of the entrance to the holy of holies indicates the superiority of this sacred chamber to the holy place. Thus, the curtains were so disposed that the nearer they came to the holy of holies they increased in richness, and in beauty, and in splendor.

The superiority of the holy of holies shown by the furniture.—In the court stood the altar of burnt offerings, overlaid with brass, and between it and the tabernacle, the laver made of finer brass, each of the serving women's mirrors. The furniture of the holy place was superior to that of the court, the shewbread table and the incense-altar being overlaid with gold, while the splendid lamp-stand was made of the precious metal itself; the furniture, however, of the holy of holies was superior to both of the other two places, the ark of the covenant being not only overlaid without like that of the table of shewbread and the altar of incense of the holy place, but also within with gold, and its cover, the mercy seat, and the cherubim of glory, of solid gold. Moreover, resting in this golden throne, and filling the space between the mercy seat and the overarching wings of the two cherubims, was the luminous shekinah cloud—the symbol of the divine presence. Thus, the nearer articles of furniture approached the holy of holies and the symbol of God's presence they increased in value, in beauty, and in significance.

The superiority of the holy of holies shown by persons.—Common people, when bringing sacrifices, and Levites, as servants of the priests, had access to the court; only priests had access to the holy place, indicating its greater sacredness and its superiority to the court; none, however, save the high priest, had access to the holy of holies, indicating its greater sacredness and its superiority to the other two places. Thus, the nearer persons came to the holy of holies and the symbol of God's presence they increased in dignity.

The superiority of the holy of holies shown by the shape of places.—The court was a double square, and open to the heavens; the holy place was superior to it as a place, for although likewise a double square, it was less incomplete as a place, being covered over; the holy of holies was superior to both of the other places, for besides being covered over it was four-square, and not only so, but formed a perfect cube, its six sides— floor, roof, north, south, east, and west walls—each measuring 10 cubits by 10. Thus, the nearer places were situated to the holy of holies and the symbol of the divine presence they became more complete as places.

The superiority of the holy of holies shown by numbers.—Four, five, seven, ten, and one hundred are numbers occurring in the tabernacle, and are frequently mentioned in the Scripture. With the exception of five, they are regarded as symbolic numbers of perfection or completeness. Five is deemed by many the number of imperfection. We prefer, however, viewing it rather as a less significant number of perfection than ten.

Court number.—The court was one hundred cubits long. There were four colors in the gate hanging. The brazen altar was four-square, and had four horns and four rings. Five was the most prominent court number. Its pillars were five cubits high, and were spaced at a distance of five cubits (Exod. 27:18). The brazen altar was five cubits long and five broad. Both the length of the court—one hundred cubits— and its breadth—fifty—were multiples of five. The five pillars from which the sanctuary door was suspended stood not in the holy place, but in the court, in the same way as the four pillars for the veil of the holy of holies stood not in that innermost chamber, but in the holy place, as a glance at the woodcut, p. 18 will show. Although the bars around the sides of the tabernacle cannot be said to belong to the court, yet they were on the outside of the sacred structure, and seen only in the court, and in this sense were identified with it. There were five of these bars along each of the sides of the tabernacle.

Tabernacle ("dwelling") numbers.—The very significant symbolic number of perfection, "ten," is prominent in the sacred dwelling, and contrasts with the prominent court number five, which, as already noticed, is deemed the imperfect number; but which we, as already mentioned, prefer regarding as a less significant number of perfection than "ten." The tabernacle internally was ten cubits high and broad. There were ten cherub curtains, and also ten goat-hair curtains, for although there was another of these goat-hair curtains, it was used entirely on the outside (p. 35). "One hundred" occurs in the tabernacle as well as in the court, that being the number of its silver

The courtyard shall be a hundred cubits long and fifty cubits wide, with curtains of finely twisted linen five cubits high, and with bronze bases (Exod. 27:18).

sockets. Four, another of the numbers of perfection, occurs in the tabernacle, and more prominently than in the court. The doors were each four-square, the roof was four-fold, four colors appeared both in the door-hangings and in the cherubim curtains. Both forty-eight, the number of the boards, and ninety-six, the number of sockets they rested on, were multiples of four. The tabernacle (dwelling) was thus, as far as symbolic numbers indicated, a superior place to the court, or if we may so speak, indicated that it was a place nearer perfection than the court.

Holy place numbers.—In this apartment was the golden altar, which was four-square, and had four rings and four horns. Here also stood the shewbread table, which had four rings; and in this sacred chamber the most significant of all symbolic numbers occurs, for here stood the splendid golden candlestick with its seven lamps and its seven-fold light. As far as numbers indicate, it is apparent that the "holy" as a place was superior to the court.

The most holy place numbers.—Here seven occurs as well as in the holy place, the blood of the sin offerings on the great day of atonement being sprinkled seven times on and before the mercy seat. Here, also, four and ten occur, and far more prominently than in the holy place. The holy place was a double square, but the holy of holies was four-square. The tops or surfaces of the brazen altar and the golden altar were four-square, but the innermost chamber of the tabernacle itself, like the same apartment in the temple, and like the New Jerusalem which John saw in vision (Rev. 21:16), was a perfect square or cube. "The length and the breadth and the height of it are equal." The holy place was ten cubits high, ten wide, and twenty long; but the holy of holies was ten cubits high, ten wide, and ten long, and every one of its sides—the roof, the floor, and the north, south, east, and west walls—was ten cubits square. Thus the holy of holies was not only a perfect square, but it was a cube formed of the very significant symbolic number of perfection, "ten." The outside of the ark of the covenant which stood in the innermost chamber does

The city was laid out like a square, as long as it was wide. He measured the city with the rod and found it to be 12,000 stadia in length, and as wide and high as it is long (Rev. 21:16).

not seem to be particularly associated with any of the numbers of perfection save its four rings; but withdraw the lid and look in, and what do you behold? The tables of stone with the *ten* commandments written on them with God's own finger. The holy of holies it is evident, as far as its numbers indicate, was the most sacred and important place of the tabernacle, and bore the most distinct marks of perfection. Let us not forget, however, in speaking of indications of greater or lesser relatively; for both the court and the holy place were planned by Jehovah Himself, and were perfectly adapted for the purposes for which they were intended. In numbers, as well as in pillars, veils, hangings, curtains, holy vessels, persons, shape of places, we have clear and unmistakable indications that the holy of holies was superior to both the court and the holy place. The nearer, as we have seen, that parts of the sacred structure, holy vessels, persons, places and numbers were situated to, or the more closely they were associated with, the symbol of the presence of the all-perfect Jehovah, they were the more valuable, beautiful, dignified, perfect in form, or significant of completeness. In this way they all distinctly pointed to the innermost apartment of the tabernacle as the region of pre-eminent beauty, perfection, and glory.

Yet this glorious throne room, and the bright shekinah cloud, were but faint types of the inconceivable and transcendent glories of the heavenly sanctuary, and of Him who there dwelleth in the light that is inaccessible and full of glory. How shall we, who are sinful dust and ashes, have access to the heavenly sanctuary, and appear before its transcendently glorious throne, when none but priests were permitted to enter even the first apartment of the tabernacle, and none but the high priest had access to the innermost chamber. Blessed be God, genuine believers are a royal priesthood, and the way of access for them into the holiest of all is open, since Christ, by His atoning death, has rent the veil in twain. No court, no brazen altar, no laver, no holy place, no golden altar, and no dividing veil now come between God's redeemed people and the heavenly throne. All that was typified by the brazen altar and the court, and by the golden altar and the holy place, are to be found in the true holy of holies. There is the Lamb of God, slain from the foundation of the world, and there is the great Intercessor, interceding for those who have believed on His name, and pleading on their behalf the efficacy of the blood which He shed for them on Calvary. Not on one day of the year, but on every day and at all times we may enter into the "holiest by the blood of Jesus, by the new and living way He hath consecrated for us through the veil, that is to say, His flesh," and there obtain mercy to pardon, and find grace to help in time of need. And while we have thus the privilege, even now, of entering the heavenly sanctuary by faith, let us be cheered by the blessed hope of its becoming hereafter the dwelling-place of our immortal souls. May every step in our earthly pilgrimage be one nearer to this happy abode, and to our Father in heaven, and one that will find us not only nearer to God but increased in meetness to stand in His presence and to serve Him day and night in His holy temple for ever and ever.

> Then let the way appear
>   Steps unto heaven;
> All that Thou sendest me
>   In mercy given;
> Angels to beckon me
>   Nearer, my God, to Thee—
> Nearer to Thee.

23
THE ENCAMPMENT AND ORDER OF MARCH

In form the encampment was square; the tabernacle occupying the central position, and the four grand divisions of the army of Israel camping around it, one on each side.

The Israelites are to camp around the Tent of Meeting some distance from it, each man under his standard with the banners of his family (Num. 2:2).

Between the Levitical tents, pitched near and around the tabernacle, and the first line of the tents of the other tribes, there was a reserved space (Num. 2:2; Josh. 3:4) regarded as holy ground, being sanctified as Mount Sinai had been, by its proximity to God's manifested presence; and, as in the case of that holy mount, death may have been the penalty for trespassing on it, or even touching it with hand or foot.

Although the Israelites were not permitted access to the space between their tents and the tabernacle for secular purposes, the prohibition did not exclude them from it when their object was to draw near God for the purpose of worship, or when called together on great national occasions. The Levites camped in the following order around the tabernacle—

Then you will know which way to go, since you have never been this way before. But keep a distance of about a thousand yards between you and the ark; do not go near it (Josh. 3:4).

On the East,
and before the gate of the court, were pitched the tents of
MOSES, AARON, AND THE PRIESTS
(Num. 3:38).

On the South Side,
the tents of the
KOHATHITES
(Num. 3:29).

The Kohathite clans were to camp on the south side of the tabernacle (Num. 3:29).

On the North Side,
the tents of the
MERARITES
(Num. 3:35).

And on the West Side,
the tents of the
GERSHONITES
(Num. 3:23).

All the men from thirty to fifty years of age who came to do the work of serving and carrying the Tent of Meeting numbered 8,580 (Num. 4:47–48).

It was a wise arrangement that this tribe should pitch its tents near and around the holy tabernacle, as the 8580 males above the age of thirty belonging to it, were the appointed ministers of the sanctuary (Num. 4:47, 48); sentinels to guard it (Num. 1:53); laborers to rear it and take it down (Num. 1:51); carriers to transport it from place to place (Num. 4); servants to assist its priests in their sacred duties (Num. 3:9); and instructors to teach the thousands of Israel that camped on every side of them. Each grand division or army of Israel was composed of three tribes, and camped as follows:—

On the East
(Num. 2:2-10),
THE CAMP OF JUDAH,
Comprising the tribes of Judah, Issachar, and Zebulun.

On the South
(Num. 2:10-17),
THE CAMP OF REUBEN,
Comprising the tribes of Reuben, Simeon, and Gad.

On the West
(Num. 2:18-28),
THE CAMP OF EPHRAIM,
Comprising the tribes of Ephraim, Benjamin and Manasseh.

On the east, toward the sunrise, the divisions of the camp of Judah are to encamp under their standard. The leader of the people of Judah is Nahshon son of Amminadab (Num. 2:3).

On the North
(Num. 2:25-29),
THE CAMP OF DAN,
Comprising the tribes of Dan, Naphtali, and Asher.

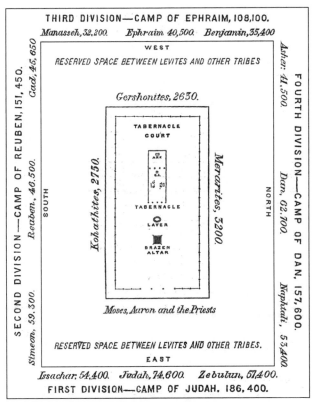

THIRD DIVISION—CAMP OF EPHRAIM, 108,100.

Manasseh, 32,200.   Ephraim 40,500. Benjamin, 35,400

WEST

RESERVED SPACE BETWEEN LEVITES AND OTHER TRIBES

Gershonites, 2630.

TABERNACLE
COURT

ARK

TABERNACLE

LAVER

BRAZEN
ALTAR

Kohathites, 2750.

Merarites, 3200.

Moses, Aaron and the Priests

RESERVED SPACE BETWEEN LEVITES AND OTHER TRIBES.

EAST

Issachar, 54,400.   Judah, 74,600.   Zebulun, 57,400.

FIRST DIVISION—CAMP OF JUDAH. 186,400.

Gad, 45,650   *Reuben, 46,500.*   *Simeon, 59,300.*

CAMP OF REUBEN, 151, 450.

SECOND DIVISION—

SOUTH

Asher, 41,500   *Dan, 62,700.*   *Naphtali, 53,400.*

FOURTH DIVISION—CAMP OF DAN, 157,600.

NORTH

Diagram of the plan of the encampment.
Dotted line indicates court wall. Dots represent the position
of the court-pillar sockets. Line next to dots indicates first lines
of Levitical tents, and the first line beyond this one, the first line
of the tents of the other tribes.

The diagram of the plan of the camp (above) will help to illustrate the preceding remarks. The encampment was square; but for want of room on the page to display it efficiently in this form, and at the same time to show the relative positions of the tabernacle, the court, the furniture, the Levitical tents, and those of the other tribes, the diagram appears as an oblong.

There were, as the diagram shows, four great camps, one on each side of the tabernacle. The camp of Judah on the east, numbered 186,400 adult males; the camp of Reuben on the south, 151,450; the camp of Ephraim on the west, 108,100; and the camp of Dan on the north, 157,600; in all 603,5500. The

Levites camped, as already noticed, on every side, between the tabernacle and the inner line of the four great camps.

The exact number of the Israelites, including women, children, and old men, is not known, but probably was about two million. The tents of so many people covered a large space, variously estimated from two to eight or ten miles square. From calculations we have made, we are certain that a square of two, or at most three miles, should have afforded ample room for the whole encampment.

The different camps, tribes, and families, had standards, flags, or ensigns to distinguish them from each other. Their banners, doubtless, differed from

How beautiful are your tents, O Jacob,
 your dwelling places, O Israel!
Like valleys they spread out,
 like gardens beside a river,
like aloes planted by the LORD,
 like cedars beside the waters.
Water will flow from their buckets;
 their seed will have abundant water.
Their king will be greater than Agag;
 their kingdom will be exalted (Num. 24:5–7).

THE FIGVRE OF THE
Tabernacle erected, and of the
Tents pitched round about it.

Given here as a curiosity from Beza's Bible, 1593.

one another, but whether in consequence of varying in color, or of having various emblematic figures embroidered on them, is uncertain, the Bible being silent on the subject.

All was arranged so as to secure the most perfect order, "Every man of the children of Israel shall pitch by his own standard, with the ensign of their father's house; far off about the tabernacle of the congregation shall they pitch" (Num. 2:2). This city of tents must have presented a most beautiful spectacle. In the center stood the tabernacle, its golden walls and silver foundation shining resplendently, and its beautiful roof-covering pointing to the heavens above, where is the "true tabernacle not made with hands." Resting upon it was the cloudy pillar, sheltering the many thousands of Israel beneath from the burning rays of the sun. "He spread a cloud for a covering," so that "the sun did not smite them by day, nor the moon by night." Around the sanctuary was the court of the Lord's house, having in the center the brazen altar, with its bright exterior, and ascending from it the curling smoke of the sacrificial victims. A beautiful wall enclosed the court, consisting of pillars and linen hangings, the silver heads and brazen feet and glittering shafts of the former contrasting to advantage with the snowy whiteness of the latter. In the court might have been seen the priests, arrayed in their robes "for glory and beauty." Near at hand, and around the tabernacle, the tents of the Levites were pitched, forming another wall of defense to the holy habitation; beyond these, on every side, stretched away the tents of the many thousands of Israel, all arranged in order, like a well laid-out city, in regular streets, and so planned, it is supposed, that each tent-door faced the tabernacle, enabling the people to worship God at their tent-doors, with their faces towards the sanctuary.

All this vast encampment, as already mentioned, was covered over by the expanded cloud—the outspread protecting wings of the Keeper of Israel. Can you doubt that the encampment of Israel in the wilderness was a scene of surpassing loveliness? Hear the description given of it by an eye-witness, who was

The divisions of the camp of Judah went first, under their standard. Nahshon son of Amminadab was in command (Num. 10:14).

sent for by a wicked and idolatrous king to curse Israel. The prophet Balaam, standing on the top of a mountain, while the camp of Israel was spread out in the plain beneath, essayed to curse Israel, but was so overwhelmed by the imposing spectacle that burst upon his view that blessings, and not curses, rolled from his lips: "How shall I curse, whom God hath not cursed? Or how shall I defy, whom the Lord hath not defied? For from the top of the rocks I see him, and from the hills I behold him: lo, the people shall dwell alone, and shall not be reckoned among the nations." "Who can count the dust of Jacob, and the number of the fourth part of Israel?" "How goodly are thy tents, O Jacob! And thy tabernacles, O Israel! As the valleys are they spread forth, as gardens by the river's side, as the trees of lign aloes which the Lord hath planted, and as cedar-trees beside the waters. God brought him forth out of Egypt; he hath, as it were, the strength of an unicorn: he shall eat up the nations his enemies, and shall break their bones. He couched, he lay down as a lion, and as a great lion: who shall stir him up? Blessed is he that blesseth thee, and cursed is he that curseth thee" (Num. 23:8–10; 24:5, 6, 8, 9).

THE ORDER OF MARCH
(Num. 10)

LEVITES,
Bearing the Ark of the Covenant
(Num. 4:15; 10:33)

ARMY OF JUDAH
(Num. 10:14–16)
JUDAH
ISSACHAR
ZEBULUN

THE MERARITES
(Num. 10:17),
with four wagons drawn by eight oxen, bearing the boards, bars, pillars, and sockets of the tabernacle, and the court pillars and their sockets

THE GERSHONITES
(Num. 10:17),
with two wagons, drawn by four oxen, bearing the
curtains, coverings, and hangings of the tabernacle,
and the hangings of the court

THE ARMY OF REUBEN
(Num. 10:18, 20)
REUBEN
SIMEON
GAD

*Then the tabernacle was
taken down, and the
Gershonites and Merarites,
who carried it, set out
(Num. 10:17).*

KOHATHITES
(Num. 10:21),
carrying the sacred furniture of the sanctuary and
the court

THE ARMY OF EPHRAIM
(Num. 10:22, 24)
EPHRAIM
MANASSEH
BENJAMIN

*The divisions of the camp
of Ephraim went next,
under their standard.
Elishama son of Ammihud
was in command
(Num. 10:22).*

THE ARMY OF DAN
(Num. 10:25-27)
DAN
ASHER
NAPHTALI

On the rising of the cloudy pillar from off the
tabernacle, the divine signal for the children of Israel
to commence their journey, they began to take down
their tents and make other needful preparations for
moving onward. In a very short time the whole camp
presented a scene of busy and exciting preparation.
As the encampment was arranged in the most perfect
order, so was the order of march. Every camp, tribe,
and family marched in the place assigned it in the
great army.

Levites, bearing aloft the ark of the covenant,
were the first to start. The ark, with the cloudy pillar
above, and perhaps tapering downwards so as to rest
on it, became a kind of sacred standard, going before
"to search out a resting-place for them." The cloud

The sons of Aaron, the priests, are to blow the trumpets. This is to be a lasting ordinance for you and the generations to come (Num. 10:8).

giving the signal, it and the bearers of the ark moved forward simultaneously. The priests now blew an alarm with the silver trumpets for the army of Judah to start; and that tribe, bearing the leading standard of the whole army of Israel, moved onward, followed by the two tribes subordinate to it—those of Issachar and Zebulun. Next came the Merarites, who had charge of four wagons, drawn by eight oxen, and laden with the boards, bars, pillars, and sockets of the tabernacle, and the pillars and sockets of the courts. Then the Gershonites, who had charge of two wagons, drawn by four oxen, and laden with the curtains, coverings, and hangings of the tabernacle, and the hangings of the court. The priests again blew an alarm, and the army of Reuben, obeying the summons, followed after the Merarites and the Gershonites. This army formed a guard to these two families of Levites, and the precious materials they had charge of. Next in the order of march were the Kohathites, carrying the furniture of the tabernacle and the court, consisting of the golden altar, the table of shewbread, the golden candlestick, the brazen altar, and the laver, all carefully covered with cloths. The army of Ephraim followed next in order, as guardians of the Kohathites and the sacred vessels of the sanctuary. And the Danite troops coming up last, formed the rearguard of the whole Israelitish host.

The Israelites must have presented a grand spectacle as they marched through the wilderness in battle array, with innumerable banners displayed and led on by the fiery cloudy pillar moving majestically in the air before them—guarding, lighting, and protecting them!

Great wisdom was displayed in the encampment and order of march. None of the arrangements were arbitrary in their nature. All was wisely ordered, and with a view to the welfare of all the tribes, and of every Israelite. We may not be able to see all the wise reasons why the army of Judah in the march led the van; and why Ephraim's occupied the third place; or why such and such tribes were grouped together; but we are able to discover as many reasons as satisfy us that each army and each tribe was assigned its place with a view to its own best interests, as well as that of the whole army of Israel.

The first place, we have already seen, was assigned to the Levites, including the priests. They camped nearest to the tabernacle, and formed a kind of outer wall of defense to it; and in the march had charge of the transport of the sanctuary and its sacred vessels. The next highest place is allotted to the tribe of Judah. It, and the two tribes subordinate to it, pitched their tents on the east and in the front, the position of greatest honor; and in the order of march preceded the other three armies—the tribe of Judah thus leading the van of the whole army of Israel. Jacob, when blessing his sons, predicted the preeminence of Judah, and the tribe bearing his name, on that account, seemed to have a right to preference; yet the tribe of Levi was more honored, in being set apart to sacred duties. This was, no doubt, humbling to the Judahites. Their being placed, however, in the forefront of the encampment, and leading the van in the order of march, may have been intended as compensation to them for the preference given to the Levites, and might well reconcile them to their position. With the tribe of Judah were associated the two tribes most closely allied to it by blood, affection, and other tender ties. Issachar and Zebulun were the descendants of Judah's two youngest brothers by the same mother. Though Judah had been predicted to the presidency of his brethren, Reuben was the first-born son of Jacob, and the tribe bearing his name, on that account, might feel that it had some claim to preference. That claim seems not to have been overlooked, for the first place is assigned it in the second great army, both in the camp and in the order of march. With the tribe of Reuben were associated those of Simeon and Gad. Simeon was Reuben's brother by the same mother, Leah, and was next to him in the order of birth, Reuben being the eldest and Simeon the second eldest son. Gad was the first-born son of Leah's handmaid. Reuben and Simeon following each other in the order of birth, and being nearly

The Levites, however, are to set up their tents around the tabernacle of the Testimony so that wrath will not fall on the Israelite community. The Levites are to be responsible for the care of the tabernacle of the Testimony (Num. 1:53).

of the same age, were in a peculiar sense near to each other, and this may partly account for the two tribes bearing their names being assorted together. It was probably in consideration of Gad's being the first-born of Leah's handmaid that the tribe descending from him is honored by being leagued with those of Reuben and Simeon, and on that account Gad would probably be the more willing to co-operate with these two. Besides forming the second army in the order of march, this one had the honor of guarding the sacred habitation and its court, as these were transported by the Levites. The third grand division of the three tribes embraced those of Ephraim, Benjamin, and Manasseh, the descendants of Jacob by his favorite wife, Rachel, so that these three tribes were more closely related to one another than to any of the other tribes, and also by very peculiar and tender ties. This grand army of Ephraim was the third in the order of march, and followed and guarded the Kohathites, who carried the sacred vessels and furniture of the sanctuary. The guarding of the golden altar, the table of shewbread, the golden candlestick, the brazen altar, and the laver, was probably deemed such an honor by the army of Ephraim as to prevent it envying the posts allotted to the other tribes.

The fourth great camp was composed of the tribes of Dan, Asher, and Naphtali, descendants of Jacob by his wives' handmaids. Of these, Dan was the leading tribe, and the army took its name from it. That Dan was appointed to the first place in one of the great armies seems to have been a recognition of the claims of the descendants of Jacob's concubines. Next to the army of Judah, that of Dan was the most numerous, and this fact was taken into account; for, next to that of Judah, it was appointed to the place of greatest danger, the rear of the whole army. If Judah's army formed the vanguard, that of Dan formed the rearguard of the great army of Israel.

How admirably, then, was each tribe assigned its place in the great encampment and in the order of march. The claims to some kinds of preference, that each one might be supposed to put forth, are duly recognized. The tribes most nearly related to one another, by blood, affection, or other ties, are grouped together, and each grand camp or army occupied the position in the encampment and order of march which it appeared to have some claim to. All seems to have been so arranged as best to promote the peace and unity and well-being of the thousands of Israel, and advance them in their journey to the promised land. The more we study the plan of the encampment and order of march, the more we admire them, and the wisdom of Him who is "wonderful in counsel, and excellent in working."

Consequently, you are no longer foreigners and aliens, but fellow citizens with God's people and members of God's household (Eph. 2:19).

Genuine believers, though seemingly disunited, are as really one as the Jewish church was in the wilderness; though they are of every color, race, and people, and dwell in all parts of the world, and are connected with various sects of professing Christians, in consequence of their not yet seeing eye to eye on all points, yet they are all one. They have been washed in the same blood, baptized by the same Spirit, and they are animated by the same heaven-inspired hopes. They are as really fellow-citizens as were those who composed the city of tents in the wilderness. They constitute but one great encampment, with the same glorious banner waving over them. They form but one great spiritual army, led on by the Captain of Salvation. They are all fellow-pilgrims marching to the heavenly Canaan, guided by a great light in the way that they are to go, even by Him who is the "light of the world."

As every Israelite and every tribe had the respective place in the encampment and in the order of march that each was to fill, appointed by God, so every New Testament Israelite has his place in the church, and in the world as well, assigned him by God, and not arbitrarily; but, as in the case of the Israelites, wisely, and with a view to his own spiritual welfare, as well as to that of the whole church.

If you are a child of God, seek ever to have a lively sense of the greatness of your privileges. They are far greater and far more numerous than were those of the Israelites. Whatever be your position in the world, and especially in the Church, remember you are where God has seen meet to place you. You are a fellow-citizen with all saints, a soldier of that great army which has Christ for its leader and commander, an heir of glory, and a pilgrim on the road to the heavenly Canaan. Ever seek to act as becometh your high calling. Do not forget that great privileges imply great responsibility and numerous duties to be performed. Whatever may be your place in the church or in the world, seek to act in both as your Captain would have you. Think not, if you are poor or unlearned, or have few talents, that there is no need for your laboring in Christ's cause, or fighting in the ranks of His soldiers. Christ has work for all His followers—has a place in His army for every true convert. If you are one, you are in the place He has allotted you, and you possess the talents necessary to fill it. Some person or persons are in the circle of your influence to an extent they are not in that of any other person. Christ demands the active exertions of all His followers. Those who bear His name, but do nothing to advance His cause, give no evidence that they are His. It is easy for some professing Christians to frame plausible excuses for not aiding by their personal efforts the Gospel cause. Indeed, the number of such is legion; but these excuses will be of no avail on the day of judgment, for to all those who professed to be Christ's, but kept aloof from His service, and were not found fighting His battles, on that day He will say, "Depart from Me, I never knew you." Suppose Judah had refused to lead the van, because Levi had been chosen to minister to the Lord; or suppose Dan had refused to being up the rear, because Judah had been appointed to lead the van; or suppose this and that Israelite refused to take the place assigned him, because associated with this or that division, would the army of Israel ever have taken possession of Canaan at all? So, in like manner, unless Christians are content to labor for the good of Zion with the means and with the talents God has given them, and in the place He has assigned them in the world and in the church, the kingdom of this world will never

The court and the cloudy pillar.

become the kingdom of our Lord and of His Christ. If you are one of those who are willingly, however humbly, laboring in the Master's service, be of good cheer, faint not by the way. You need not. You have divine strength to support you, and an unerring Guide to conduct you in the path of duty. If you bend your ear to Him, you may ever hear His encouraging voice saying, "My grace is sufficient for thee; for My strength is made perfect in weakness." Turn you eyes towards Him, and you may ever behold Him, as a great light walking before you, and beckoning you onward in the way you are to go—a good way, a way leading to victory, glory, honor, and immortality. "Be thou faithful unto death, and I will give thee a crown of life."

24
THE CLOUDY PILLAR

Then the angel of God, who had been traveling in front of Israel's army, withdrew and went behind them. The pillar of cloud also moved from in front and stood behind them (Exod. 14:19).

From the day the tabernacle was reared in the midst of the Israelites till the day they crossed the Jordan, the cloud of the Lord was inseparably associated with this portable temple of the Most High, resting upon it right above the ark of the covenant while the pilgrim Hebrews encamped in the wilderness, and moving in the air above the ark while they were on the march, and as it was being carried in the journeys through the desert.

Of all the manifestations of God's gracious presence vouchsafed to His ancient people, the cloudy pillar was the most striking and glorious. There was only one pillar—the same that was a pillar of cloud by day being a pillar of fire by night. In this respect resembling the smoke which, ascending the air from furnaces, has the appearance of cloud by day and of fire by night. A still better illustration, perhaps, is the contrivance adopted by some generals, and amongst them by Alexander the Great, of causing a lofty pole to be set up, and on its summit to be placed a brazier filled with combustible materials, kept ever burning over the general's tent when encamped, and in the forefront of the moving host when on the march—"a cloudy banner by day, a flaming beacon by night."

Besides being designated the cloudy pillar, it was occasionally called by the following names:—

1. *The angel of God.*—It was so-called as other inanimate objects serving God's purposes are sometimes designated in the Bible (Exod. 14:19).

2. *The Lord.*—The pillar served the purpose of enveloping or enshrining the shekinah, a bright refulgent flame, the symbol of God's presence with His people. The symbol, as it stood for God, is occasionally regarded as God and called by His name: "The Lord went before them in a pillar of cloud, to lead them the way" (Exod. 13:21).

3. *God's throne.*—The cloudy pillar was God's moveable throne while the Israelites were on the march; His stationary throne while they were encamped, resting, as we have already indicated, on the top of the sacred tent, right above the ark. A portion of the inner bright flame, the shekinah, penetrating down through the roof of the tabernacle, filled the space between the mercy seat and the overarching wings of the cherubim that stood one on each end of the golden throne: "Give ear, O shepherd of Israel, thou that leadest Joseph like a flock; thou that dwellest between the cherubim, shine forth" (Ps. 80:1). God, as represented by the shekinah, was thus enthroned in the cloudy pillar *without* the tabernacle, and on the ark of the covenant *within* the sacred dwelling.

When the tabernacle had to be taken down, preparatory to the Israelites removing to a new place of encampment, that portion of the mystic flame resting on the ark of the covenant ascended into the cloudy pillar, which now enshrined the entire Shekinah. As soon as the Levites bearing the ark had taken their place in the forefront of the host, the cloudy pillar took up its position in the air right above this the most sacred of all the objects pertaining to the tabernacle. The cloud and the ark being thus inseparably associated, accounts for the people being represented as following sometimes the one and sometimes the other.

The cloudy pillar served many useful purposes.

First, It was a guide.—To lead was its main mission: "The Lord went before them by day in a pillar of cloud to lead them the way, and by night in a pillar of fire to give them light, to go by day and by night" (Exod. 13:20–22). Imposing in height, and having the appearance of cloud by day and of fire by night, it rose conspicuous to view in the dark night and received the implicit obedience of the many thousands of Israel.

> When Israel, of the Lord beloved,
>   Out from the land of bondage came,
> Their father's God before them moved,
>   An awful guide, in cloud and flame!
> By day, along the astonished lands,
>   The cloudy pillar glided slow;
> By night, Arabia's crimsoned sands
>   Returned the fiery column's glow.

When it move forward they followed, and when it stood still they halted and encamped beneath its sheltering wings. It ever guided in the right way, however much it seemed sometimes to be otherwise. Apparently it led in the wrong direction when the Israelites began to march under its leadership, causing the people to encamp in a situation of extreme danger; thus tempting their enemies to pursue and all but overtake them (Exod. 13:20–22; 14:1–13). It was, however, the right way after all, as the pilgrims, when they saw the salvation of God, acknowledged in a triumphal song (Exod. 15:1–21). While the pillar was leading the Israelites to Pi-hahiroth on the Red Sea, and through that sea, and up and down wadies, and into the neighborhood of implacable foes, even all the way through the great and terrible wilderness, it was ever an unerring guide: "He led them forth by the right way" (Ps. 107:7), and "He led them on in safety, so that they feared not" (Ps. 77:53). The pillar was a striking illustration of the long-suffering kindness of our Heavenly Father. Neither murmurings, nor rebellions, nor idolatry, nor ingratitude, ever drove away the angel of His presence. "He took not away the pillar of the cloud by day, nor the pillar of fire by night, from before the people" (Exod. 13:22). The guidance vouchsafed was of the most gracious kind. It was like that of a shepherd. "He made His own people to go forth like sheep, and guided them in the wilderness like a flock" (Ps. 78:52). Nor like the guidance of a shepherd only, but like that of a loving and

Then the Lord said to Moses, "Tell the Israelites to turn back and encamp near Pi Hahiroth, between Migdol and the sea. They are to encamp by the sea, directly opposite Baal Zephon. Pharaoh will think, 'The Israelites are wandering around the land in confusion, hemmed in by the desert.' And I will harden Pharaoh's heart, and he will pursue them. But I will gain glory for myself through Pharaoh and all his army, and the Egyptians will know that I am the Lord." So the Israelites did this (Exod. 14:1–4).

*Then Moses and the Israelites sang this song to the Lord:
"I will sing to the Lord, for he is highly exalted. The horse and its rider he has hurled into the sea" (Exod. 15:1).*

affectionate parent: "The Lord thy God bare thee, as a man doth bear his son in all the way that ye went" (Deut. 1:31). The pillar led all the way from Egypt, and only disappeared when it had accomplished its mission by bringing the pilgrims safely and triumphantly to the end of their journey.

Second, It was a light.—Had the pillar not changed its aspect when the sable curtains of evening gathered around the Israelites, it would have become invisible. As soon, however, as day departed and night set in, it became a bright shining and resplendent column, a fiery pillar, visible to every eye; serving now not only to guide, but also to illumine, and whether the army camped or marched, ever gave a cheery light. The hours of night in the terrible wilderness would have been very dismal save for the friendly light shed around the chosen people by the fiery pillar: "The pillar of the cloud departed not from them by day to lead them in the way; neither the pillar of fire by night to show them light, and the way wherein they should go" (Neh. 9:19).

Third, It was a shade.—He spread, we are told, "a cloud for a covering" (Ps. 105:39). Only those who have wandered in deserts, exposed to the scorching sun of the East, can form an adequate idea of the comfort afforded by this grateful awning. The head of the pillar spread out to such a wide extent as to overshadow the Israelites when they were encamped as well as when they were on the march, so that the sun did "not smite them by day, nor the moon by night" (Ps. 121:6).

Fourth, It was a shield.—In Deut. 1:30, we read, "The Lord your God which goeth before you, He shall fight for you." Salvation was sure to the Israelites when the angel pillar interposed between them and their foes. The most signal instance of its acting as a shield occurred at the Red Sea. Soon after Pharaoh had allowed the children of Israel to depart from Egypt, repenting that he had permitted them to go, he followed with great armies, and came in sight of the pilgrims as they were camping at Pi-hahiroth by the Red Sea. When the Israelites saw the Egyptians they

The LORD your God, who is going before you, will fight for you, as he did for you in Egypt, before your very eyes (Deut. 1:30). and in the desert. There you saw how the LORD your God carried you, as a father carries his son, all the way you went until you reached this place (Deut. 1:31).

He spread out a cloud as a covering, and a fire to give light at night (Ps. 105:39).

were greatly alarmed; the air was rent by their terror-stricken cries. They saw no possible way of escape—the deep, broad sea stretching out before them, their enemies seeking their immediate destruction close behind, and just about "to make of them their prey," while high mountains bristling with frowning fortresses rose on this side and on that, rendering escape impossible in any direction. Their extremity was God's opportunity, for at this awful and critical moment, enthroned in the cloudy pillar, He moved quietly, swiftly, and majestically from before the Israelites and went behind them, and there stood an impenetrable shield between them and the Egyptians. The side of the pillar towards the Egyptians was so black as to plunge them into total darkness, but the side towards the Israelites so bright as to flood them with glorious light, and to shed its golden sheen across the rippling wavelets.

The cloud was thus both a sun and a shield to the people of God. The Egyptians could not reach the chosen people because of the pillar cloud. Though thus protected by this almighty shield, they could not continue where they were. They must proceed on their journey. "Speak," said God to Moses, "unto the children of Israel, that they go forward." Forward through the great deep sea? Yes! Moses now stretched his hand, with his rod in it, over the sea, and immediately the waters divided and stood up like two great crystal walls, one on their right and one on their left, leaving a broad, dry road between. On that hitherto untrodden path the Israelites, lighted by the friendly pillar, passed over safely and triumphantly to the other side, while Pharaoh and his proud captains in their war chariots looked on in dread amazement. Hardening his heart yet once more, and deeming the dry road as good for him as for the people of God, with his captains and warriors he descended into the great gap between the solid sea walls in hot pursuit after the escaping Israelites. The Egyptians, however, had not gone far, when looking up they saw the pillar now in the air above them, assuming an awfully wrathful aspect: The Lord God of battles was looking

down in anger upon them. They were troubled, and
well they might be. Moses again stretched out his rod,
and the congealed sea-walls, obedient to the mystic
wand, at once melted, and, rushing impetuously forward to meet and embrace each other, engulfed as in a
great whirlpool the doomed Egyptians. Not a single
soul escaped: "they sank as lead in the mighty waters."
By nature we all stand on the margin of a great Red
Sea, but as Moses by his rod, so Christ by His cross, has
made a way through the great Red Sea of sin and guilt
for His believing people to pass over to the better land.

Guided thus safely by the fiery pillar across the
Red Sea, and on to the shores of Arabia, Moses and
the saved people sang a song of triumph. The women
were led by Moses' sister. Miriam the prophetess took
a timbrel in her hand, and all the women followed her
with timbrels and with dances; and well might those
feet dance on the dry land which had passed dry-shod
through the mighty deep.

> Sound the loud timbrel o'er Egypt's dark sea!
> Jehovah has triumphed, His people are free;
> Sing! For the pride of the tyrant is broken,
> His chariots and horsemen all splendid and brave;
> How vain was their boasting the Lord hath
> but spoken,
> And chariots and horsemen are sunk in the wave;
> Sound the loud timbrel o'er Egypt's dark sea,
> Jehovah has triumphed, His people are free!

Thus the pillar was a shield. Had it not come
between the Israelites and their enemies at the Red
Sea, and guided them safely through the deep waters,
instead of being thus gloriously delivered, they must
have perished by the sword of the Egyptians or been
drowned in the Red Sea.

Fifth, It was an oracle.—In the cloudy pillar, we
are told in Exod. 33:9, "the Lord talked with Moses"—
phraseology easily comprehended, when we take into
account the close connection between it and the
shekinah, somewhat analogous to that between the
spirit and the body. It is not improbable when the
Lord spake unto Moses face to face, as a man
speaketh unto his friend, that the inner resplendent

As Moses went into the tent, the pillar of cloud would come down and stay at the entrance, while the LORD spoke with Moses (Exod. 33:9).

flame of the shekinah was manifested to him. In the ninety-ninth Psalm we are told, "He spake unto them in the cloudy pillar." From this oracle sounded forth words necessary for the direction and instruction of the congregation. He who opened His mouth in the burning bush at Horeb opened His mouth in the cloudy pillar, and spake to Israel's leader for Israel's welfare.

During the last watch of the night the LORD *looked down from the pillar of fire and cloud at the Egyptian army and threw it into confusion (Exod. 14:24).*

Sixth, It was an avenger.—When the Lord wished to make known His displeasure, the cloudy pillar assumed a very wrathful appearance. The Lord, we are told, "looked through the pillar of fire and of the cloud, and troubled the host of the Egyptians" (Exod. 14:24). What an awful aspect it must have worn when flashes of fire went forth from it and devoured Nadab and Abihu (Lev. 10:2). And also when fire came out from it and consumed 250 men, as we are informed in the sixteenth chapter of Numbers. If the aspect of the pillar was thus at times such as to trouble those with whom God was angry, it wore a very pleasing aspect towards His obedient people. As they looked up to the pillar they beheld the shining face of their Divine Leader, cheering and encouraging them to go forward in their journey as He directed. He is called by this very name "face." "If Thy presence (Heb. "face") go not with me, carry us not up hence" (Exod. 33:15).

So fire came out from the presence of the LORD *and consumed them, and they died before the* LORD *(Lev. 10:2).*

Such, then, were some of the ends served by the fiery cloudy pillar. It was a guide, a light, a shade, a shield, an oracle, an avenger. It led, it illumined, it shaded, it shielded, it spoke, it smiled, it frowned. It showed the way, and beckoned to the thousands of Israel to follow. It turned the darkness into light. It warded off the darts of the noonday sun. It was a bulwark of defense between the Hebrews and the Egyptians. It fought for the chosen people. When pleased it rewarded, and when provoked it punished. It continued it friendly guidance, its light, its protection, its counsel, and its encouragement, until it conducted the many thousands of Israel safely across the Jordan and into that good land and large, the promised land of Canaan. Of all the objects ever seen by the Hebrew pilgrims this was the grandest, the

And fire came out from the LORD *and consumed the 250 men who were offering the incense (Num. 16:35).*

most imposing, and the most resplendent. Greatly privileged were the people to whom it was vouchsafed. To them, and to them only, pertained the "glory."

Typical and Spiritual Significance

The Christian pilgrim is favored with no such visible manifestation of the Deity as he travels through the wilderness of this world to the heavenly Canaan. He must hold on his way without ever seeing with bodily eye "the glory," and without ever hearing the audible voice of Him who spake in the cloudy pillar. Are the privileges, then of the children of God less under the gospel dispensation than were those of the Hebrews under the Mosaic one? By no means. In reference to this very cloudy pillar, there are glorious predictions respecting New Testament Israelites: "And the Lord will create upon every dwelling-place of Mount Zion, and upon her assemblies, a cloud and smoke by day, and the shining of a flame of fire by night; and upon all the glory shall be a defense" (Isa. 4:5). "Arise, shine; for thy light is come, and the glory of the Lord is risen upon thee" (Isa. 60:1).

The fiery cloudy pillar was the dispenser mainly of temporal blessings, and was itself temporary in its nature, and so passed away. But the blessings promised in the above texts are spiritual and everlasting.

Although the people of God in our day do not see Christ their Shekinah Pillar Cloud with the bodily eye, they see Him with the eye of faith.

> Though now unseen by outward sense,
> Faith sees Him ever near.

And He is even more graciously present now, than He was to the Israelites in the cloudy pillar, for the dimness of types and shadows has for ever passed away, and the true light now shineth. The Moon of the Old Testament is succeeded by the glorious Sun of the New.

Christ and the Cloudy Pillar

Christ is to the Christian pilgrim what the cloudy pillar was to the Israelites,

1. Like the Cloudy Pillar, Christ Is a Guide

First, He guides by His example.—He says, "I am the way." As long as we walk in the path made by His own blessed footsteps we shall not lose the road to glory. Christ, like the pillar, goes before this people, and says to them, "Follow Me." Marching after Him, every step will bring us nearer the better country. When assailed by temptations, like Him, let us place the tempter behind our back; when badly used, let us like Him not revile again. Like Him let us go about continually doing good, for in being imitators of Jesus, we will make progress in our heavenward journey, and in our meekness for the inheritance of the saints in light. Christ prayed often. Before break of day He climbed the solitary mountain to have communion with His Father. Let us early in the morning follow His steps up the mount of devotion, and we shall be refreshed as He was with gracious blessings coming down upon our souls from Him who hath said, "I will be as the dew unto Israel," and we shall descend as He did, renewed in strength for the work of the day, and resolving so to engage in its duties, that our souls may be benefited and God glorified. Spending the day thus, we shall at its close, "pitch our tents a day's march nearer home."

Second, Christ guides by His Word.—"Thy word is a lamp unto my feet, and a light unto my path" (Ps. 119:105). "When thou goest it shall lead thee, and when thou awakest it shall be with thee, for the commandment is a lamp and the law is a light" (Prov. 6:22,23). The Bible, like the angel pillar, is an ever present and seen guide. We can see it with our bodily eyes, and even feel it with our hands, and open it where we may, discern it ever pointing onward and upward. If we follow its guidance, we will not miss the way, nor fail to reach at last the blessed shores of Canaan.

Third, Christ guides by the Holy Spirit.—Whom He has promised to send to His people in order to guide them into all truth (John 16:13).

By these and other agencies Christ, our Pillar Cloud, leadeth ever in the right direction, even when like the cloud He may seem to be acting otherwise. Into whatever circumstances of difficulty, suffering, or danger He may bring His people they need not have the slightest fears, for He is a divine and unerring Leader. Be strong in faith ye whose believing eyes are fixed on Jesus, your Pillar Cloud; and even should unscalable mountains appear to rise between you and the land to which you are traveling, or should great and impassable deeps seem to intervene between you and it, be assured, that though the road looks like the wrong way, it is the right one after all. "Though He slay me yet will I trust in Him" (Job 13:15). "Yea, though I walk through the valley of the shadow of death, I will fear no evil, for Thou art with me; Thy rod and Thy staff they comfort me" (Ps. 23:4). "None can stay [Thy] hand, nor say unto [Thee], What doest Thou?" (Daniel 4:35). It is well for us that we cannot stay Thy hand, for if we could and did, we would be staying a hand that is always doing good, and never evil; doing good even when it seems to us to be doing evil.

All the peoples of the earth are regarded as nothing. He does as he pleases with the powers of heaven and the peoples of the earth. No one can hold back his hand or say to him: "What have you done?" (Dan. 4:35)

2. Like the Cloudy Pillar, Christ Is a Light

"I," says He, "am the Light of the World." Till illumined by Him none can see. It is His office to pour celestial light on the eyes of the spiritually blind. It is the same great light that chases away our darkness, and enables us to see the first step of our spiritual pilgrimage, that brightens our path during all the succeeding steps of our journey to the heavenly Canaan. We can miss the way or stumble on the road only if we willfully shut our eyes, and refuse to admit His glorious rays.

> The way is dark, the storm is loud,
>> The path no human strength can tread;
> Jesus, be Thou the pillar cloud,
>> Heaven's light upon our path to shed.

John the Baptist, as well as all other burning and shining lights, only reflected the beams of the Sun of Righteousness, who "lighteth every man that cometh into the world," and who is not only the light of the world, but of heaven as well. "The city hath no need of the sun, neither of the moon to shine upon it, for the glory of God did lighten it, and the lamp thereof is the Lamb" (Rev. 21:23, RV).

3. Like the Pillar Cloud, Christ Is a Shade

To pilgrims traveling heavenward, he is "the shadow of a great rock in a weary land" (Isa. 32:2), for while He screens from the burning sun of this busy, bustling, honor and pleasure-seeking world, they are preserved from being withered and scorched by its fiery and deceitful rays. Were this blessed shelter, provided by a gracious Savior to all who trust in Him, withdrawn, how soon would all that is lovely and pure and God-like in their souls be burned out. Favored by this gracious protection they may so engage in this world's business and affairs as not to retard but promote their heavenward journey.

While within the shadow cast by a present and gracious Savior they are safe; it is only when wandering beyond into forbidden paths that their souls are in danger.

> But present still though now unseen
> When brightly shines the prosperous day,
> Be thoughts of Thee, a cloudy screen,
> To temper the deceitful ray.

4. Like the Pillar, Christ Is a Shield

He said to Paul, and still says to every one of His disciples, "My grace is sufficient for thee; for My strength is made perfect in weakness" (2 Cor. 12:9). Defended by His grace, the fruitful may ask, "Where are the enemies who can overcome the righteous?" If Christ come between them and the legion of foes ever seeking the destruction of their souls, are they not as safe from the assault as were the Hebrews from the Egyptians at the Red Sea, when the cloudy pillar stood between the pursuing and the pursued? Weak at the best are Christians in themselves, as the Israelites would have been had they been left to themselves at Pi-hahiroth. The Christian's strength lies in his knowing his own weakness, which prompts him to lay hold of an almighty shield able to defense in every emergency. However many and strong the enemies may be that are bent on the ruin of his soul, he has but to look away from himself and up to Him in Whom "all fullness dwells," and as he looks, trustingly to exclaim, "My sufficiency is of Thee," in order to be effectually guarded, and to experience that when he is weak then is he strong. His soul is exposed to the darts of the enemy only when he neglects to interpose between it and them this almighty armor. Guarded by it, he may sing, "The Lord is . . . my buckler" (Ps. 18:2), "my refuge and my fortress; my God; in Him will I trust" (Ps. 91:2).

5. Like the Pillar, Christ Is an Oracle

"He is the Word," the grand medium of communication between God and man. No man hath seen God at any time, "the only-begotten Son who is in the bosom of the Father, He hath declared Him" (John 1:18). "God who at sundry times, and in divers manners, spake in times past unto the fathers by the prophets, hath in these last days spoken unto us by His Son" (Heb. 1:1, 2). Let us lend our ears to this great Oracle, our Savior Christ, and listen and give due heed to His commandments, and we shall become wise unto salvation, and receive all necessary direction for our journey through this wilderness world to the heavenly Canaan.

6. Like the Pillar, Christ Is an Avenger

Christ, like the wondrous cloud, looks with a smiling face on His people; like it, however, he also looks with an angry countenance on His and their enemies. And while He is not willing that any should perish, but that all should repent, believe and be saved, He it is that shall pass the awful sentence of condemnation on the finally impenitent: "Depart from Me ye cursed into everlasting fire, prepared for the devil and his angels."

Christ is thus as real as the fiery cloudy pillar that went before the Hebrews, a Guide, a Light, a Shade, a Shield, an Oracle, an Avenger, a fast Friend, and a constant Attendant. Like it He leads, He enlightens, He screens, He shields, He defends, He instructs, and He commands.

The Israelites on the march to the land of promise are a type of the Christian on his journey through this world to heaven. Jesus is the glorious Shekinah Pillar Cloud that goes before him all the way to the better land. Fix but your eyes on Him, and you will find Him more precious to you than was the friendly pillar to the Israelites. It led them like a shepherd; and if you are led by Him you are following the Good Shepherd, and can claim Him as your own, and say: "The Lord is my Shepherd." It led them into pleasant places of encampment, and so will He lead you:

> The Lord's my Shepherd, I'll not want,
>   He makes me down to lie
> In pastures green; He leadeth me
>   The quiet waters by.

At the Jordan the cloud took its departure. It did not accompany the Israelites into Canaan, but Christ will never leave those whom He has guided through the wilderness of this world to the land of bliss.

> The Lamb which dwells amidst the throne
>   Shall o'er them still preside;
> Feed them with nourishment Divine
>   And all their footsteps guide.

Once under the guidance of Jesus, Christian pilgrims have nothing to fear. His promise is: "I will never leave thee, nor forsake thee." Blessed Jesus, if Thou forsake us not, then be the way ever so beset with enemies, ever so impeded by barriers, and be the trials and sorrows and privations ever so many and great, we will not fear, for in spite of these and all other hindrances Thou will lead us on in safety, and we shall reach home at last.

> My Father's house on high,
>   Home of my soul, how near
> At times to faith's foreseeing eye,
>   The golden gates appear.

Not all who marched after the fiery cloudy pillar were privileged to enter the land of Canaan; many

. . . and the ransomed of the LORD will return. They will enter Zion with singing; everlasting joy will crown their heads. Gladness and joy will overtake them, and sorrow and sighing will flee away (Isa. 35:10).

perished by the way on account of their sins; but none of Christ's followers ever perish on the road to glory; all of them, the least as well as the greatest, the feeblest as well as the mightiest, hold on to the end of their Christian pilgrimage, and after crossing the Jordan, enter the heavenly Canaan in triumph, "with songs and everlasting joy upon their heads" (Isa. 35:10).

APPENDIX

Prefatory Note

The following chapters, forming an appendix are numbered and paged in continuity to those of the body of the work for the sake of simplicity and reference.

Though the subjects are all of a controversial nature, we have endeavoured to make our treatment of them interesting and easily understood. A glance at the table of contents below will show that they are all less or more closely connected with the Tabernacle. We trust our readers will be enabled by what we have advanced to form an independent opinion on the various points in dispute.

25

THE HEBREW CUBIT

A great diversity of opinion exists, even among expert Biblical scholars, as to the length of the Hebrew cubit. Almost every one of the writers whose articles appear in our chief Biblical encyclopedias comes to a different conclusion. One states the length to be 16 inches (*Biblical Educator,* Vol. 2, p. 280); another, 21 inches (*Kitto's Cyclopædia,* Vol. 1, p. 501); another, 19.0515 (Rev. W. Latham Bevan, M.A., *Smith's Bible Dictionary,* Vol. 3, pp. 1736–39); while other writers give other lengths, varying from 16 to 25 inches.

Biblical cubits—There are three cubits, each of a different length, mentioned in the Bible:—

First, The cubit after the cubit of a man (Deut. 3:11). *Second,* The modern or later cubit, implied in the cubits after the first (former, old, or ancient) measure (2 Chron. 3:3). *Third,* Ezekiel's great cubit (Ezek. 41:8). He speaks of six great cubits, and his great cubit is defined to be a "cubit and an hand breadth" (Ezek. 40:5).

Which of these three was the one in general use by the Hebrews, and according to which are the measurements of Noah's ark, the tabernacle, and Solomon's temple, and their furniture? The writers in *Smith's Dictionary of the Bible,* under weights and measures, contends—(1) that the former, old or ancient measure (2 Chron. 3:3), was the Mosaic or legal cubit; (2) he holds that the modern measure, the existence of which is implied in the above passage, was one somewhat longer; (3) he says the cubit after

(Only Og king of Bashan was left of the remnant of the Rephaites. His bed was made of iron and was more than thirteen feet long and six feet wide. It is still in Rabbah of the Ammonites.) (Deut. 3:11)

The foundation Solomon laid for building the temple of God was sixty cubits long and twenty cubits wide (using the cubit of the old standard) (2 Chron. 3:3).

I saw that the temple had a raised base all around it, forming the foundation of the side rooms. It was the length of the rod, six long cubits (Ezek. 41:8).

I saw a wall completely surrounding the temple area. The length of the measuring rod in the man's hand was six long cubits, each of which was a cubit and a handbreadth. He measured the wall; it was one measuring rod thick and one rod high (Ezek. 40:5).

It was a handbreadth in thickness, and its rim was like the rim of a cup, like a lily blossom. It held two thousand baths (1 Kgs. 7:26).

It is to be square—a span long and a span wide—and folded double (Exod. 28:16).

A champion named Goliath, who was from Gath, came out of the Philistine camp. He was over nine feet tall (1 Sam. 17:4).

These are the measurements of the altar in long cubits, that cubit being a cubit and a handbreadth: Its gutter is a cubit deep and a cubit wide, with a rim of one span around the edge. And this is the height of the altar: (Ezek. 43:13).

a man (Deut. 3:2) is held to be the common measure in contradistinction to the Mosaic, and to have fallen below the latter in point of length.

We agree with this writer when he says that the former or ancient measure (2 Chron. 3:3) was the Mosaic or legal cubit, but we disagree when he says that this was not the measure "after the cubit of a man." There can be no doubt, both from the testimony of Scripture and Josephus, that the Mosaic or legal cubit of the Hebrews and the cubit "after the cubit of a man" were one and the same. As to the new or modern cubit, implied in 2 Chron. 3:3, we have no data either in Scripture or elsewhere to enable us to find, or even to try to find out, its length.

The cubit "after the cubit of a man" we recognize as the Mosaic or legal cubit, according to which are the measures of Noah's Ark, of the tabernacle and Solomon's temple and their furniture. It seems strange to us that any should doubt this, seeing that other measures taken from members of the human body are used in connection with Hebrew measurements, such as an handbreadth (Exod. 25:25; 1 Kings 7:26; 2 Chron. 4:5), and span (Exod. 28:16; 39:9; 1 Sam. 17:4; Ezek. 43:13).

Approximate Length of the Cubit after the Cubit of a Man

Cubit, derived from the Latin *cubitus*, the forearm, the bone, anatomically from the elbow to the wrist; but as used anciently, and without reference to anatomy, from the elbow to the tip of the middle or long finger. If men were all of equal height, and the members of their bodies of equal length, there would be no difficulty in determining the length of the cubit; but, as this is not the case, we have to try to find out the most likely average by which the Hebrew cubit was fixed.

Eighteen Inches the Most Likely Average Length

By measuring the forearm, the handbreadth, and the span of several men, we find the average to be: the cubit, 18 inches; the handbreadth (the four fingers held close together), 3 inches; the span (the distance from the tip of the thumb to that of the little finger, and consisting of three handbreadths), 9 inches. Accordingly,

3 inches . . . . make 1 handbreadth.
9 inches or 3 handbreadths, ... make 1 span.
18 inches or 2 spans, ... make 1 cubit.

The writer is a man of medium height. In measuring his forearm he finds it to be 18 inches, his span to be 9 inches, and his handbreadth to be 3 inches. All these three measures were employed in the measurements of the tabernacle and Solomon's temple, as we have seen.

Josephus uses span for half-a-cubit. The average length of the span, as we have shown, is nine inches. Any one who likes to try will find that the average length cannot be more than nine inches. Those learned scholars, therefore, who hold the length of the Hebrew cubit to be 21, 22, 23, or 25 inches, notwithstanding their labored studies of the indications of the length of a cubit (as applied to that of a Hebrew cubit) in the tombs and monuments of Egyptian and Babylonian antiquities, must be mistaken.

Josephus, as we have seen, employs the span as equal to half-a-cubit, which shows that the usual cubit of the Hebrews was that of a cubit after the cubit of a man, and also that the cubit could not have exceeded eighteen inches [*Antiquities*].

Where the Bible text speaks of two cubits and a-half, Josephus speaks of five spans; when the Bible text speaks of a cubit and a-half, he speaks of three spans, showing that the cubit after the cubit of a man was that adopted by the Hebrews:

Have them make a chest of acacia wood—two and a half cubits long, a cubit and a half wide, and a cubit and a half high (Exod. 25:10).

Exod. 25:10.	Josephus 3.6, 5.
The Ark.	The Ark.
"Two cubits and a-half shall be the length thereof, and a cubit and a-half the height thereof."	"There was also an ark made, sacred to God . . . length five spans, breadth and height three spans."

The Great Cubit Of Ezekiel

consisted of a cubit (as we understand the cubit of a man) and an hand breadth (40:5)—together 21 inches —according to which were the measurements of his ideal temple. It is thought he adopted this great cubit from the Babylonians. Be this as it may, those are wrong who suppose that it was this great cubit (of 21 inches) that was employed in the measurements of the tabernacle and Solomon's temple, for there is nothing in Scripture or in Josephus to show that this was the case, but the reverse.

The conclusion, therefore, to which we come is that the length of the Hebrew cubit in use by the Jews in the measurements of the tabernacle and Solomon's temple was equal to eighteen of our inches, at all events approximating nearer to this measure than to any other number of inches.

In proof of our contention, we quote the following statement from an article in Vol. 24, pp. 483, 484 of the *Encyclopædia Britannica*, "The pre-Greek examples of this cubit in Egypt give 18.23 inches as a mean...This cubit, or one nearly equal, was the Siloam inscription." According also to the barleycorn measurement, the length of the Hebrew cubit approximates nearer to 18 inches than to any other number of inches.

Barleycorn Measurement

The Jews and Mohammedans had a system of measurement by barleycorns, according to which 1 digit or finger-breadth was equal to 6 grains; 4 finger-breadths or 1 hand-breadth, equal to 24 grains; 6 hand-breadths, or 1 cubit, equal to 144 grains.

As grains vary in size, it is not very easy to arrive at the length of the cubit by this system of measurement. It is the breadth, and not, as some suppose, the length, of the grains that is measured, consequently grains require to be placed side by side, and not end to end, when being measured.

Writers on the Subject

(1.) A writer in the *Penny Cyclopædia* (Vol. 27, p. 198) was at great pains in getting grains from various quarters. Those of which he speaks in the following paragraph appear to us to be those which were fairest for the trial. The grains were placed side by side. He says: "On trying the first grains we obtained, we found, that by picking out the largest grains, thirty-three of them just gave more, and thirty-two less, than 5 inches; but that, taking the grains as they came, thirty-eight gave only 5 inches." As this ratio of thirty-eight average grains gives 5 inches, 144 (the number in a cubit) gives 18.947 inches.

(2.) Colonel C. M. Watson, C.M.G., R.E., in *Palestine Exploration Fund Quarterly Statement, July,* 1897. The Colonel has gone very minutely and carefully into the study of this subject. He says, "Having been unable to find any work upon the subject—that the length of the cubit as based upon the width of the barleycorn, had been carefully investigated—I procured some ordinary Syrian barley from Jerusalem, and having cleared them of husks, made a scale of the grains about 30 inches in total length. The grains were placed exactly touching each other, with the axes parallel, and were glued down, so as to remain perfectly firm, and thus enable careful and repeated measurements to be taken." The result of his most careful and painstaking measurement is that the Hebrew cubit was 17.70 inches.

The computations of these two writers come surprisingly near to each other.

The Length of the Hebrew Cubit
According to 144 barleycorns.

	Inches.
As computed by writer in *Penny Cyclopæia*,	18.947
As computed by Colonel Watson,	17.70

The mean of these two computations is 18.323^1/$_2$ inches. Thus the length of the Hebrew cubit, computed according to the barleycorn system of measurement as well as to that of the cubit "after the cubit of a man," approximates more nearly to 18 than to any other number of inches.

26

CONJECTURES AS TO THE BREADTH OF THE HOUSE

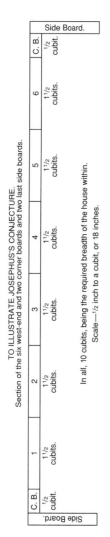

TO ILLUSTRATE JOSEPHUS'S CONJECTURE.
Section of the six west-end and two corner boards and two last side boards.

In all, 10 cubits, being the required breadth of the house within.
Scale—½ inch to a cubit, or 18 inches.

As to getting the width of the six west-end boards and the two corner boards to make up exactly ten cubits, the required internal breadth of the tabernacle:

JOSEPHUS'S CONJECTURE.—"As to the wall behind where the six pillars (boards) make up together only nine cubits, they make two other pillars (boards) and cut them out of one cubit, which they placed in the corners" (*Ant.* 3:6, 3).

Objections to Josephus's conjecture.—First, The corner boards are so placed that they cannot properly be called corner boards. *Second,* and chiefly, it makes the corner boards only one-third of the breadth or size of an ordinary board, whereas the text states that the corner boards had each two tenons, and for these there were two sockets as well as for each of the other boards, implying that they were equal to the rest. The sockets were all a talent weight each.

DR. KALISCH'S CONJECTURE.—"The larger sides consisted, therefore, of twenty such boards, whilst the shorter (western) were to contain eight boards. But the latter would not cover a breadth of ten but of twelve cubits. It is therefore added that six boards shall be made for the side westward, and other two for the corners of the tabernacle in the two sides, they shall be double beneath and above it at the two corners. From this obscure passage it appears in our opinion that each board was half-a-cubit thick, so that six boards at this western end would completely close the tent from within (nine cubits added to one-half cubit at each side, being the thickness of the boards at the northern and southern wall, make ten cubits). One-half cubit breadth is double at each corner, and one-half cubit stands over at each side" (*Commentary*, p. 366).

Objections to Dr. Kalisch's conjecture.—First, Instead of ten cubits as required, it only gives a breadth of nine cubits to the house within. Dr. Kalisch is mistaken in thinking that he has solved the difficulty regarding the corner boards and the size of the house, for when he speaks about the measurement and disposition of the curtains, he bases rightly his calculations on the internal breadth of the house being ten cubits, which is contrary to his own conjecture (pp. 366, 367). *Second,* Half-a-cubit (nine inches) is far too great a thickness for the boards.

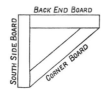

Section of south-west corner.
From Mr. Pressland's model.

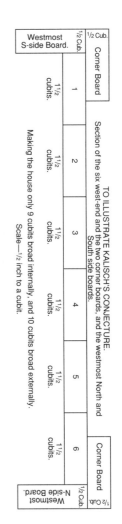

Mr. Pressland of London is quite wrong in supposing that he has solved the difficulty arising out of the corner boards, for in his model tabernacle only six boards are comprised in the breadth of the house, making it only nine cubits broad internally. A corner board is placed at each corner in the inside of the house so as to form with the side and back-end board a kind of triangle at each corner.

According to this conjecture, the holy of holies, which was ten cubits high, could not be a perfect square or cube like that of the same apartment in the temple, and in that of the New Jerusalem, which John saw in vision, "The length and the breadth and the height of it" would not be equal.

GERLACH'S CONJECTURE.—"That the boards were one cubit thick" (*Commentary on the Pentateuch*).

This conjecture gives both the required breadth and length of the house within, which neither that of Pressland or Kalisch does. But the fatal objection to it is that the boards are at least three or four times too thick, and their weight out of all proportion to that of the sockets they rested on. The weight of each such board—

	cwts.	qrs.	lbs.
If of acacia wood	18	3	12
If of beech or ash	18	1	4
If of fir or pine	9	1	4

Even allowing that the wood of which the tabernacle was constructed was very light, is there the least probability that a board would weigh about half-a-ton, when the two sockets it rested on weighed only 93 lbs. 12 oz. each?

OUR OWN CONJECTURE.—We venture to hazard the following solution of the difficulty, believing it to be better than any other that has been brought forward. We have given it at p. 13, but repeat it here so that it may be more easily compared with the others: —That the boards were one-quarter of a cubit or four and a-half inches thick. That the corner ones were angular in shape, each consisting of two equal halves of an ordinary board, dovetailed or otherwise united, yet so as, when united, to have constituted one board. That one-half of each faced respectively the south and north sides (see diagram).

By this conjecture one-third (half-a-cubit) of each corner board, together one cubit is added to the breadth of the house, making with the nine cubits of the six back boards ten cubits, the desired breadth of the house. Each at the joining below and above was further bound or coupled together by a ring or staple; or the meaning of the text may be that the staple or ring joined, coupled, or bound them to the boards next to them on both sides. The text is very obscure (Exod. 26:23, 24): "Two boards shalt thou make for the corners; and they shall be coupled together beneath, and they shall be coupled" (Heb. "twins") "together above the head of it into one ring" (from a Hebrew word signifying "to dip"); "thus shall it be for them both, they shall be for the two corners."

Our own conjecture has the following advantages to recommend it—(1) The internal length and breadth of the house are as required—thirty cubits long and ten cubits broad; (2) The boards are of a

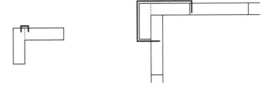

Ring or staple dipping into corner board (the one prong into the one twin and the other prong into the other twin), where two halves have been jointed into one board.

Ring or staple if intended to join or couple corner boards to the boards on each side of them.

reasonable thickness; (3) the corner boards are real corner boards; and though one-half of each laps over the last side boards, the symmetry of the framework is not thereby destroyed, as a glance at the diagrams will show, while this lapping over tends to compact the structure at the corners, and makes the thickness at these important points double. These corner boards have a connection both with the side and back walls, and are the means, along with the rings, of laying hold of the three walls and binding them into one; thus, besides their mere position, they differ in a peculiar and important sense from the other boards, and are well entitled to the name "corner boards;" (4) The text is illustrated. There is a sense in which these corner boards, each consisting of two halves, yet when united, forming but one whole, may be called "couples," "pairs," or "twins," or which, when clasped at the foot and at the top by a ring or staple as illustrated above, may be said to have been "coupled together" and also "to the boards next to them."

27

THE SURPLUSAGE OF THE CHERUBIM AND GOAT-HAIR CURTAINS

In the cherubim curtains there is a large surplusage not easily accounted for (p. 27), and in the goat-hair curtains there is a corresponding surplusage (p. 30, 31). As stated at p. 31, which we repeat here, the five goat-hair curtains of the grand division of six spanned the roof, and hung down the walls of the holy place, being the exact measure required; and half of the other grand division of five curtains spanned the roof, and hung down the walls of the most holy place; and the remainder of this great curtain (may this not be the half curtain of Exod. 26:12?) hung down the back wall, being the exact length required to reach the ground, yet leaving a large surplusage as indicated in the diagrams, p. 27 and p. 30.

As for the additional length of the tent curtains, the half curtain that is left over is to hang down at the rear of the tabernacle (Exod. 26:12).

Dr. Kalisch tells us that the half of this grand division of five curtains hung down the back wall, but ignores the fact that one-third of it was sufficient for the purpose. While trying to solve lesser difficulties, the doctor finds it convenient to take no notice whatever of the superfluous two-thirds which measures 10 feet by 20, nor of the corresponding surplusage of 10 feet by 18 in the cherubim curtains, yet affirms that he has solved all the difficulties arising out of the apparent discrepancy between the measurement of the wooden frame-work and the curtains.

Soltau, in his *Tabernacle and the Priesthood*, at p. 48, says:—"Half the curtains which was formed of the five breadths of four cubits joined together, hung down over the back or west end of the tabernacle so as to cover up that extremity, for the width of it would be exactly twenty cubits; ten of which would reach over the top, from the taches to the end of the tabernacle, and other ten would fall down from the top over the west end, so as to reach to the ground." He forgets all about the length of the curtains which was thirty cubits, and while using up all the width of the curtains, uses up only a third of the length. Moreover, a third of the other half of this great curtain of five breadths was used for the roof of the holy of holies, so that not an inch of the half Mr. Soltau referred to was required for the roof.

Otto Von Gerlach, in speaking of the goat-hair curtains, although unlike Dr. Kalisch and Soltau, not blind to this large surplusage, gets easily over the mountain of difficulty by remarking that the half of the great curtain (of five) hung down the back wall *in folds,* leaving it to be inferred that the superfluity was used up by this means. A very easy mode of getting quit of a superfluity, two-thirds more than was necessary to hang down, and not only so, for besides there was the similar surplusage in the cherubim curtains.

Mr. Fergusson, the celebrated architect (*Smith's Bible Dictionary,* p. 1451), asserts that he has solved all the difficulties which have troubled former restorers; but while the sloping-roof of his tabernacle effectually uses up the entire curtains, it gives rise to a very large deficiency (a greater difficulty than that of a surplusage), besides creating other difficulties greater than those which he vainly attempts to solve (see p. 203, 204).

We admit our inability to solve the difficulties arising out of the surplusage in both sets of curtains, but these are difficulties that no one else as yet has solved.

28

MR. FERGUSSON'S SLOPING ROOF TABERNACLE

(*See his article under "Temple" in* Smith's Bible Dictionary.)

The sloping roof tabernacle of Mr. Fergusson may make a finer picture than a flat-roofed one; this, however, is not the point to be decided. We maintain that there is not a single word in the text giving the slightest hint about a ridge-pole and its supports which are involved in a sloping roof, and besides, as Mr. Fergusson himself shows, the boards and the pillars require to be double the number of those mentioned in the text in order to suit a sloping roof. Yet, notwithstanding all this, several learned men (see appendix, chapter 29) have adopted Mr. Fergusson's roof without testing its merits, or caring whether it was scriptural or not; hence we deem it not unnecessary to devote a chapter to this subject.

Before, however, examining his arguments in favor of a sloping roof, let us look for a little at those by which he attempts to demolish a flat one.

First, he says: "The tent had a ridge, as all tents from the days of Moses down to the present time have had." This is a mere assertion, not having a single passage of Scripture in support of it. It may be true of tents in general, but it does not follow that this portable temple must in this and every other respect have resembled them. The text gives the most minute particulars of the curtains, skins, boards, and pillars, and even of the loops, taches, hooks, and pins; but not a single word or hint is given in it about a ridge-pole and its supports, both of which are involved in a sloping roof.

Second, Mr. Fergusson asserts that the arrangement of the curtains (for a flat roof) is in direct contradiction to the Scriptures. We are told there, he says (Exod. 26:9), "that half of one of the goat-hair curtains shall be doubled back in front of the tabernacle, and only the half of another (verse 12) hung down behind, and (verse 13) that one cubit shall hang down on each side, whereas this arrangement makes ten cubits hang down all round except in front." In reply to this, observe—(1) Exod. 26:9 does not say that a half, but a whole curtain was doubled in the forefront of the tabernacle; (2) ten cubits of cherub curtains hanging down the sides is not inconsistent with the text, the object being to explain what was done with the two additional cubits in the length of the goat-hair curtains, and which says that one cubit of these, at both sides, shall hang over the sides of the tabernacle (cherubim curtains), and so covering the blank space between the foot of these cherubim curtains and the ground. If the cubit on each side hung, according to his theory, as a fringe, it would cover no defined space, and hence not agree with the text, which distinctly states it was used for a covering.

Third, Mr. Fergusson tells us, that "every drop of rain falling on the tabernacle would fall through." It had a fourfold roof—(1) the linen curtains; (2) the goat-hair ones, which were impervious to the rain; (3) the rams' skins, of which, however, Mr. Fergusson says: "with the wool on, and when wet, would depress the center;" but he has no scriptural authority for this statement, and the probability is that the wool was off (see p. 32); and (4) the badgers' skins. How could every drop of rain fall through such a roof as this? "However tightly," Mr. Fergusson says, "the curtains might be stretched, the water would never run over the edge." The breadth to be spanned was only fifteen feet, and there was nothing to prevent the skin coverings from being so stretched as to render the roof quite flat, and to admit of rain running over the edges. We have stretched a piece of waterproof cloth across a model tabernacle, fastening it down to the tops of the boards, and have both rained and poured water upon it, and not a single drop fell through. The most of the water ran over the edges; a little was left on it owing to its level surface, which probably would be the case with respect to the tabernacle in the wilderness when it rained (if it ever rained), were there no simple contrivance to run it off; but before what might be left on the roof could penetrate through the fourfold covering, would it not be absorbed by the atmosphere of a "thirsty land"?

... the sun will not harm you by day, nor the moon by night (Ps. 121:6).

Fourth, Mr. Fergusson, not content with having every drop of rain falling through a flat roof, adds: "While snow falling on such a roof would certainly tear it to pieces." Admitting that snow sometimes falls on the mountains of Sinai, it seldom, if ever, falls in the wadies and plains; and if slight showers do occur, they are like angels' visits, few and far between. Few of the authors we have followed across the desert seem to have observed snow falling. The Israelites, who were in the habit of complaining of privations, never once complained of snow-storms. In the midst of snow falling it must have been difficult to distinguish or gather the manna that fell every morning. But, granting that snow did fall occasionally, would the 8000 able-bodied Levites, who camped around the tabernacle, and whose duty it was to care for the sacred structure, not be able to remove what might alight on the roof, by unfastening the covering, and shaking the snow off, or even by some more easy method? But with respect to both rain and snow-storms, supposing there were any during the journey —which is doubtful—would not the outspread cloudy covering which screened the Israelites from the burning rays of the sun (Ps. 105:39; 121:6), also shield them from weather that might otherwise have been hurtful to them?

Fifth, All tents having had ridges from the days of Moses, every drop of rain falling through the flat roof and snow tearing it to pieces, one would think were sufficient to completely demolish it; but no: Mr. Fergusson has another weapon in reserve—viz., the middle bar (Exod. 26:28), with which he deals it its death-blow; that blow, however, will be considered presently.

Having now witnessed the wished-for wreck of the flat roof, we direct particular attention to the sloping one which Mr. Fergusson raises on its ruins. He asserts that the tabernacle had a sloping roof; that the middle bar (Exod. 26:28, 36:33) was its ridge-pole; that the linen and goat-hair curtains did not hang down the walls, either on the inside or the outside, but with the skins, formed the roof only, which extended 5 cubits beyond the walls, not only in front and rear, but on both sides.

They made the center crossbar so that it extended from end to end at the middle of the frames (Exod. 36:33).

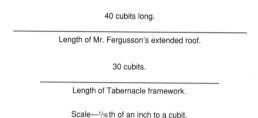

40 cubits long.

Length of Mr. Fergusson's extended roof.

30 cubits.

Length of Tabernacle framework.

Scale—¹⁄₁₆ th of an inch to a cubit.

The length of this extended roof is 40 cubits, and the depth of each of its slopes 14 cubits (together 28 cubits), being the exact measurement of the cherubim curtains, so that its two slopes and the dimensions of the curtains agree. There were eleven of the goat-hair curtains, one more than there were of the fine linen ones. Mr. Fergusson says the half (although the text says the whole) of this additional

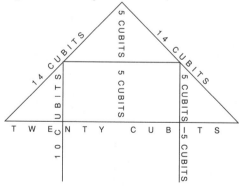

Section showing sloping roof; each slope 14 cubits deep.
Scale—¹⁄₈th of an inch to a cubit.

curtain was doubled up in the forefront of the tabernacle, the other half, about a yard, hanging down as a fringe behind. These curtains were also two cubits longer than the linen ones, and were placed

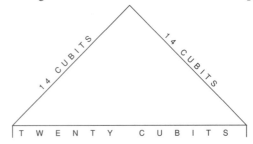

Section showing cubit of goat-hair curtains hanging over cherub curtains, according to Mr. Fergusson's roof.
Scale—1/8th of an inch to a cubit.

lengthways down the sloping roof, a cubit on the one side, and a cubit on the other side, hanging over the cherub curtains (see diagram). The ridge-pole was supported at the east end on the middle pillars at the entrance to the habitation, and at the west end on the middle board, which, he tells us, was raised five cubits above its fellows, for this purpose (and which, he says, there is nothing to contradict), and also on a pillar situated five cubits beyond the west wall, where, he informs us, there "was at least one pillar; there may have been five." Only half of the curtains, Mr. Fergusson informs us, were used within; the other

Mr Fergusson's tabernacle as restored.

half, on the outside, formed the ceiling of verandahs on every side of the erection. The front verandah, not being enclosed, constituted the porch; and the side and back ones, probably being enclosed, were used as cloisters for the priests.

Such, then, is a brief outline of Mr. Fergusson's proposed restoration of the tabernacle; and we shall now apply to it the test of Scripture, and especially so, as he maintains that it is in strict conformity with every word and every indication of the sacred text.

The center crossbar is to extend from end to end at the middle of the frames (Exod. 26:28).

Objections to Mr. Fergusson's Restoration of the Tabernacle

First, The text does not furnish the ridge-pole. It is easy for Mr. Fergusson to say (in order that he may find a pole) "five rows of bars are quite unnecessary, besides being in opposition to the words of the text." Nothing, however, he advances proves this assertion. Both texts in which the bars are mentioned (Exod. 26:28; 26:33) plainly teach that there were five bars arranged in so many rows. The middle bar is evidently one of these five, for it is not named till after they are noticed, and then it is not said, "Thou shalt make a middle bar," but, "the middle bar in the midst of the boards shall reach from end to end." As to five rows being unnecessary, we have only to say that if one row tended to compact the boards, five rows would do so more effectually.

Mr. Fergusson tries to get Josephus to help him to turn this middle bar into a ridge-pole. He quotes for this purpose the following paragraph: "Every one of the pillars or boards had a ring of gold affixed to its front outward, into which were inserted bars gilt with gold, each of them five cubits long, and these bound together the boards, the head of one running into another, after the manner of one tenon inserted into another. But for the wall behind, there was only one bar that went through all the boards into which one of the ends of the bars on both sides were inserted" (*Antiquities* 3.6,3). "So far," says Mr. Fergusson, "everything seems certain and easily understood." The very reverse, however, is the case.

Anyone reading this extract would understand Josephus to say that each board had only one ring attached to it, and that there was only one row, consisting of five short bars, running along each of the two side walls, and but one bar running along the back wall. Josephus, however, does not say any one of these three things, as anyone may see by turning up the passage. Mr. Fergusson plainly misquotes the Jewish historian in his labored effort to give birth to a pole. But, even assuming the extract correct, it will not serve his purpose, although, after quoting it, he remarks, "So far, therefore, everything seems certain and easily understood." If at each long side there was only one row consisting of five short bars, of course there was no necessity for the narrow back wall having a row consisting of five short bars; and hence, Mr. Fergusson makes Josephus say, quite consistently, "Bur for the wall behind there was only one bar." But then, are we to believe the Scriptures, which say there were five bars for the back wall, or Josephus (as quoted by Mr. Fergusson), who says there was but one? The placing of these five bars at the narrow back wall completely overturns Mr. Fergusson's theory, and proves that there were five bars, arranged in five rows along each of the three walls. But he goes a little further, for, instead of giving the one bar, or middle bar, to the back end, as he makes Josephus do, he transports it into the air, and in its upward flight metamorphoses it into a huge ridge-pole!

The difficulty of transporting bars forty-five feet long across the wilderness, Mr. Fergusson thinks, is against the supposition of their being that length. But these bars may have consisted each of two or more parts, and yet have been but single bars. A fishing rod may consist of several and yet be but one rod. Even supposing this had not been the case, would a huge ridge-pole, fifteen feet longer, have been less unwieldy and more easily transported? But we must not forget that he is the parent of the pole, and hence the partiality with which it is treated, as, witness the following passage in which, while hinting at some of the difficulties connected with it, he diminishes these by reducing the length of his own pole: "No pole could be made stiff enough to bear its own weight and that of the curtains over an extent of forty-five feet without internal supports." Now, the extent of his extended roof is much greater than this, as he tells us elsewhere, and as the woodcut of the south-east view of the tabernacle restored shows (p. 196). There we see ten curtains, each four cubits broad, spread over it, and the ridge-pole extending the whole length of forty cubits, or sixty feet. We cannot account for Mr. Fergusson contradicting himself as well as the text, on any other hypothesis than this, that when he views the supposed difficulties connected with the theories of others he looks through a powerful magnifier, and when he views those connected with his own creations, he looks through as powerful a diminisher. Second, the additions to, and alterations made on, the framework by Mr. Fergusson, in order to get it to bear up the said ridge-pole, have not a single text, or even hint, in Scripture in their support.

Hang the curtain from the clasps and place the ark of the Testimony behind the curtain. The curtain will separate the Holy Place from the Most Holy Place (Exod. 26:33).

He supports the pole by resting it on the middle backboard (to the stature of which he adds five cubits that it may answer this purpose), and on a pillar of his own inventing, which he places five cubits behind the back wall, "there may," he says, "have been five pillars there." What text warrants him to add to the height of any board, or to add one or five pillars to the number of those mentioned in the text? There must have been pillars beyond the back wall, Mr. Fergusson tells us, because the Scriptures, in speaking of the back, always speak in the plural, "the two sides westward."

If you examine the text, however, you will find that it is not a row of pillars and the six west-end boards that constituted the sides westward, but only the six west-end boards themselves, whatever the meaning may be. The plural seems to be used in a metaphorical sense.

Half of the back wall having traversed the south side of the house and the other half the north side, seems to be the reason why these six boards are called sides. This view is borne out by the consideration that in the Hebrew the word translated "sides," as applied to the back wall, is different from that rendered "side" for the north and south walls. In Hebrew, that for the back wall is "thighs." If you draw an imaginary line right up the center of the ground-plan of the tabernacle, you will see this illustrated.

The length of Mr. Fergusson's extended roof is forty cubits. Where, then, was the center door pillar situated? Was it separated from its neighbors, and placed five cubits farther east from the threshold of the sanctuary, that the end of the pole might rest on it, as the woodcut of his tabernacle restored shows? If so, then it was employed for a different purpose than that which the text states it was made for. Or, were the whole five removed five cubits east? If so, then the hanging that was suspended from them would be a door, not to the sanctuary, but to the assumed porch. Or, if the five pillars were situated where the Bible places them, then the middle one could not afford a rest to the end of the ridge-pole. We apprehend Mr. Fergusson is shut up to the necessity of placing an additional pillar—perhaps five—at the east end as well as at the west end.

The tent curtains will be a cubit longer on both sides; what is left will hang over the sides of the tabernacle so as to cover it (Exod. 26:13).

The middle board being raised five cubits, besides being unscriptural, has a burden imposed upon it out of all proportion to that which its fellows had to bear, yet its socket was of the same weight as theirs. But Mr. Fergusson may reply, "Perhaps a few talents of silver were added to it." It would be as scriptural to add five talents to a socket, as five cubits to the height of a board.

Third, It is extremely unlikely that only half of the cherubim curtains were displayed within the sanctuary. Mr. Fergusson places only the half of the beautiful cherubim curtains within the sanctuary; the other half he disposes on the outside, and which, he says, formed verandahs on every side. The front, not being enclosed, is the porch; the back and side ones he would fain believe were enclosed, and accordingly he encloses them with boards (see woodcut, p. 196), thus more than doubling the number of boards mentioned in the text. "That at least the back verandah was enclosed," he says, "must have been the case, as this back place is called *Mishcan,* or the 'dwelling,' as distinguished from *ohel,* or the tent, which applies to the whole structure." This certainly is a great mistake. No back verandah, or back place, at the outside of the sanctuary is either mentioned or called Mishcan in the text. It is the cherubim curtains as a whole that are so called (Exod. 26:1, 7, 12, 13; 35:11; 36:13; Num. 3:25–36). And why are these beautiful cherub curtains called the tabernacle or dwelling? Because they went to form cloisters for the priests to dwell in? Surely not; they were evidently so named because they were everywhere visible within—on the roof above and on all the walls—and thus pre-eminently constituted the dwelling-place of Israel's Divine King.

Tent of Meeting, the curtains of the courtyard, the curtain at the entrance to the courtyard surrounding the tabernacle and altar, and the ropes—and everything related to their use (Num. 3:25–26).

Turn to the third chapter of Second Chronicles, and in imagination enter the temple, which was made after the model of the tabernacle, and what do you behold? Look up; the ceiling is adorned with cherubim. Look at the walls on both sides; cherubim there too. Behold the veil before you, all over with the same symbolic figures. Enter the tabernacle and view it as we have disposed of the curtains, and you will see that ceiling, walls, and veil, as far as these mystic figures are concerned, correspond with those of the temple, of which the tabernacle was the prototype.

They were responsible for the care of the ark, the table, the lampstand, the altars, the articles of the sanctuary used in ministering, the curtain, and everything related to their use (Num. 3:31).

Mr. Fergusson says: "The only tangible reason for supposing that the sides were enclosed is, that the temple of Solomon was surrounded on all sides except the front by a range of small cells five cubits wide, in which the priests resided, who were specially attached to the service of the temple." It can easily be shown that this is a very intangible reason, and that all the indications of the Scripture are against the supposition. The tents of the tabernacle priests were

*Then he said to me, "The
north and south rooms
facing the temple courtyard
are the priests' rooms,
where the priests who
approach the LORD will
eat the most holy offerings.
There they will put the
most holy offerings—the
grain offerings, the sin
offerings and the guilt
offerings—for the place is
holy. Once the priests enter
the holy precincts, they are
not to go into the outer
court until they leave
behind the garments in
which they minister, for
these are holy. They are
to put on other clothes
before they go near the
places that are for the
people" (Ezek. 42:13–14).*

situated close by, even before the door of the courts, and the space between their tents and the tabernacle was considered holy ground, so that their dwellings were, in a sense, within the sacred enclosures; hence there was no necessity for cloisters being made for them against the sides of the tabernacle. But further, some of the purposes the temple cloisters served,— such as being places for the priests robing and unrobing, and for eating the portions of the sacrifices that fell to their lot (Ezek. 42:13, 14)—were also served by the holy place in the tabernacle (Lev. 16:23), proving beyond a doubt that there were no enclosed places at the sides of the sacred tent.

Mr. Fergusson is shut up to the necessity of inventing cloisters for the tabernacle, as his extended sloping roof cannot do without enclosing boards. It was impossible for a cubit of goat-hair curtains on the one side, and a cubit on the other side (Exod. 26:13) to hang over the soft linen curtains (according to his disposition of them) which had no bars or hard substance at their termination, and hence he doubles the number of boards mentioned in the text in order to suit his extended roof, and that "the cubit of goat-hair curtains on each side" might have something to hang over against.

Fourth, The difficulty arising out of the apparent discrepancy between the dimensions of the framework and those of the curtains is not solved by the sloping roof.

Mr. Fergusson makes very short work of the opinions of those who differ from him, when he supposes the text will not bear them out, by remarking that this or that arrangement "is in direct opposition to the words of Scripture." Is it not strange, then, that with such professed reverence for the sacred text, he should take such liberty with it himself—as adding five cubits to the height of a board, transforming a bar into a huge ridge-pole, placing a pillar (perhaps five) beyond the back wall, giving to the tabernacle a porch and verandahs, and enclosing the latter with boards? All this is not strange at all, if we put faith in him, for he tells us that he takes all these liberties "in strict conformity with every word and every indication of the sacred text." If he treats the sacred text in this manner, may not any other restorer do the same, and add on, five, or ten cubits to one, two, three, or more boards, or add five, ten, or twenty to the number of pillars, or transform a bar into a pillar or something else, or lay a burden on a part which it was never designed to bear, and then say that he takes all these liberties in strict conformity "with every word and every indication of the sacred text"? But Mr. Fergusson will not allow this; he will suffer no one to vary even a single letter from the text or make any alteration whatever that deviates a hair's breadth from its indications. These are privileges he reserves for himself alone.

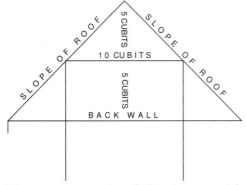

The greatest wonder of all is that, notwithstanding all his alterations, additions, and transformations, and contradictions of the text, he has not succeeded in getting the dimensions of the curtains to agree with those of even his own sloping-roofed tabernacle.

According to his own showing, the curtains are entirely used up by the two slopes of his roof, not a rag is left to cover the open space at the back, forming a triangle which has a base measuring twenty cubits and a depth from the apex to the center of the base of ten cubits. The reach, also, from the top of the back boards to the top of the ceiling, is five cubits. Would the rain and snow with which Mr. Fergusson batters down the flat roof not drift through these great open apertures into the interior, even into the holy of holies? Nor was there a rag left to cover the open spaces of a similar triangle at the east end.

Whatever, then, may be the difficulties connected with a flat-roofed tabernacle, they are infinitesimal in comparison with those of the sloping-roofed tabernacle of Mr. Fergusson.

29

THE DEAN OF CANTERBURY AND PROFESSOR MILLIGAN ON THE TABERNACLE

Some may be of opinion that too much has been said about Mr. Fergusson's sloping-roofed tabernacle, but as his long, able, and elaborate article in Smith's *Dictionary of the Bible* is in defense of the tabernacle having had such a roof, we do not see how we could have sufficiently and satisfactorily replied to it in fewer words. When an article appears in such a work as the above, and claiming to be written by one who is supposed to be pre-eminently qualified for the task, it sometimes happens that other learned men, writing on a similar topic, look up to him as an authority, and adopt his views without testing their merits or even taking the trouble to try to understand them. This is exactly what has occurred with respect to Mr. Fergusson's "Restoration of the tabernacle." The Very Reverend R. Payne Smith, D.D., Dean of Canterbury, having read Mr. Fergusson's article, gets very confused notions into his head about the structure, and while in this state of mind he writes an article on the subject in a work in which, if anywhere, we might expect to obtain the latest and best information on Bible themes. The following are a few extracts from his contribution to the *Bible Educator:*—

"Vol. 1, p. 80.—Taking the cubit as equal to 18 inches, the ark was 3 feet 9 inches in length and 2 feet 3 inches in height and breadth. This alone stood in the holy of holies, a small chamber 18 feet square." It was 10 cubits square, and taking the cubit at 18 inches it was 15 feet and not 18 feet square.

Then Solomon said, "The LORD has said that he would dwell in a dark cloud" (1 Kgs. 8:12).

Dr. Smith proceeds: "And always, except on the march, so covered that all was dark within. Into this solemn gloom once in a year the high priest entered alone."

It is true the Lord said (1 Kings 8:12) "that He would dwell in the thick darkness," but this was referring to the chamber being entirely without natural or artificial light. This sacred place in the tabernacle was not "all dark within," for the Lord, by a visible symbol, was enthroned on the mercy seat, and that symbol was a resplendent light or flame, and would surely shed some light in the throne-room. Neither the light of the sun, nor the seven-fold light of the golden lamp-bearer, shone in the innermost apartment, and as far as they were concerned it would have been in utter darkness, but it had a more glorious light than either in Him who shone forth from between the cherubim. Surely the region where God manifested His gracious presence, and which was a type of that place where *there is no night,* could not be one of darkness nor of *solemn gloom.*

"The Holy Place," says the Dean, "was of the same breadth as the Holy of Holies, but twice its length, itself carefully covered over, but lighted with the seven-branched candlestick, and containing also the table of shewbread, the altar of incense, and the altar of burnt offering."

If it was all dark and solemn gloom in the holy of holies it is clear the dean gives us a superabundance of light in the holy place, for besides the seven-fold light of the splendid lamp-bearer, the fire of the brazen altar and that of burning bullocks blazed here. We cannot conceive how the tabernacle and all that it contained could have been prevented from being burned to the ground.

"These two chambers," says the Dean, "were made of movable boards, two feet three inches broad, and fifteen feet high, fastened to sockets of silver, while over all four coverings were thrown; not lying flat upon them as many have supposed, but supported by a ridge-pole raised thirty feet above the ground in front, and the coverings were so arranged that a passage of seven feet six inches was left between the boards forming the walls of the inner shrines and the edge of the curtains." The space between the boards was not seven feet six inches, but fifteen feet.

Mr. Fergusson invents, as we have seen, boards to rest or take hold of the edge of the curtains; but the Dean does not inform us how he supports the edge of the curtains. He says the ridge-pole was raised above the ground in front. He appears not to understand in the least what he is saying, for he speaks of the ridge-pole as if it were a flagstaff. He seems to think it quite unnecessary to tell us in what part of the text we are to find it, and the internal supports which it involves. Mr. Fergusson raises this imaginary pole to a height of twenty-two and a-half feet (fifteen cubits) above the ground; but his disciple, Dr. Smith, not content with even this high elevation, raises it to a still greater height, even to thirty feet (twenty cubits). As we have seen (p. 203), every inch of the curtains was used up by Mr. Fergusson's sloping roof, so that they could not have been nearly long enough for the two slopes of a roof whose ridge-pole was seven and a-half feet higher than his. In fact, for such a roof there was no more cloth than to suffice for one of its slopes, and for about half of the other one, and to cover the large triangular spaces at the front and back, there was not even a rag. Mr. Fergusson takes the liberty of adding five cubits to the stature of the tabernacle, but the Dean of Canterbury goes a great deal further, for he adds ten cubits to the height of the sacred structure; and both writers think it quite scriptural to do so without any warrant whatever from the Bible. "These coverings," continues the Dean, "were four in number the first of fine twined linen, of various colors, embroidered with cherubim, and formed into curtains six feet wide and thirty-seven feet in length. Over these was a covering of goats' skins, consisting of eleven curtains, each six feet wide and forty feet long."

Seeing that a ridge-pole raised thirty feet above the ground would require a greater extent of curtains than for any other "Restoration of the tabernacle" that has been designed yet, one would have thought

*Make the tabernacle
with ten curtains of finely
twisted linen and blue,
purple and scarlet yarn,
with cherubim worked into
them by a skilled craftsman
(Exod. 26:1).*

that the restorer would not have diminished the length of the curtains; but this is what the very Reverend Dean has done. The fine linen curtains were twenty-eight cubits or forty-two feet long—not thirty-seven; and the other curtains were not of goats' skin, but of goat-hair, and were thirty cubits or forty-five feet long, and not forty feet as incorrectly stated. No light, but a flood of darkness is thrown on the tabernacle by this article in the *Bible Educator.* It cannot be better described than in the author's own words, "All is dark and solemn gloom, a gloom so dense as not to be pierced by even one ray of light."

The late Rev. William Milligan, D.D., Professor of Divinity and Bible Criticism in the University of Aberdeen, after describing the tabernacle, says, at p. 42 of the third volume of the *Bible Educator,* "The diagram (p. 41) will sufficiently illustrate what has been said;" and also very properly remarks, "It (the tabernacle) was all to be executed in strict accordance with the Divine directions, and nothing was to be left to merely human ingenuity or skill." And yet the diagram which illustrates his observations is, in almost every particular, opposed to the text of Scripture, and is entirely according to human ingenuity or skill— (1.) The diagram represents the structure with a ridge-pole, which is a mere human invention, or at least a mere conjecture, for not a single word is said about it or its supports in the text. Although it is one of the most important features in the above diagram, yet the professor is silent on the point, and remarks, "The directions for the construction of all parts" (of the tabernacle) "are given in the Old Testament with unexampled minuteness; the directions extending not only to its leading parts, but to the smallest particulars —the loops of the curtains, the hooks of the pillars, the rings of the bars, the cords, and the pins." What about the ridge-pole and its supports? (2.) This imaginary pole in the diagram is raised ten cubits (fifteen feet) above the tabernacle boards, or twenty cubits above the ground. We have already shown conclusively, by diagrams and otherwise, that for a sloping roof supported by a ridge-pole at this elevation, there

*Make curtains of goat
hair for the tent over
the tabernacle—eleven
altogether. All eleven
curtains are to be the
same size—thirty cubits
long and four cubits wide
(Exod. 26:7–8).*

was not nearly enough of goat-hair curtains, not an inch being left over after forming the two slopes, either to enclose the large triangular space above the door hanging, or that above the boards at the back-end. (3.) Mr. Fergusson admits that a ridge-pole involves at least one pillar to support it at each of its extremities, besides other internal supports; but the ridge-pole of the tabernacle in the *Bible Educator* (Vol. 3, p. 41) has no such pillar to bear it up. Of course the text does not furnish any, nor any other supports whatever. It is difficult to conceive how the ridge-pole could rest on nothing, when it is made to sustain the whole weight of the curtains and skin coverings. (4.) Twelve curtains are represented in the diagram as constituting the slopes of the roof, whereas there were only eleven goat-hair curtains altogether. (5.) While the court is properly represented as twice the length of its breadth, the tabernacle itself, which was three times its breadth, is represented in the diagram as only half its proper length. It may make a better picture than if its length had been shown to be three times that of its breadth, but in this and other respects which we have pointed out, the text is not in the least cared for. Everything is left, to use Professor Milligan's own words, "to merely human ingenuity and skill."

Whether our remarks on Mr. Fergusson's sloping roofed tabernacle and on other details of the structure, may or may not be of use to general readers, they may not be altogether valueless to learned men and others who are ignorant of these details, and yet lecture and write articles and even books about them. If the Dean of Canterbury, whether he agreed with our views or not, had spent an hour in looking into our little work, he certainly never would have crowded so many blunders together as are to be found on p. 80 of volume I of the *Bible Educator*.

30

THE PEREGRINATIONS
OF THE GOLDEN CANDLESTICK

Make a lampstand of pure gold and hammer it out, base and shaft; its flower-like cups, buds and blossoms shall be of one piece with it. Six branches are to extend from the sides of the lamp-stand—three on one side and three on the other. Three cups shaped like almond flowers with buds and blossoms are to be on one branch, three on the next branch, and the same for all six branches extend-ing from the lampstand. And on the lampstand there are to be four cups shaped like almond flowers with buds and blossoms. . . .

Titus evidently thought he had secured a rare prize in the golden candlestick, seeing he caused it to be conspicuously exalted in the triumphal procession to Rome (p. 68), where, some time after, he had it honorably placed in the temple of Peace, in which it remained in honor and safety for the long period of four centuries.

In Carthage.—In the year A.D. 455 Rome was conquered by the Vandals under Genseric, their king, who transferred the golden candlestick to Carthage (see Gibbon's *Decline and Fall,* chapter 36).

Again in possession of the Romans.—After remaining eighty-three years in Carthage the golden candlestick, on the Vandals being conquered by the eastern army of the Romans under Belisarus, again came into the possession of the Romans, and was taken by the victorious general to Constantinople, the then eastern capital of the empire (Gibbon's *Decline and Fall,* chapter 41).

Restored to Jerusalem.—The Emperor Justinian generously restored the precious relic to Jerusalem, where it found a resting-place in the Church of the Holy Sepulcher. Gibbon remarks: "And the holy vessels of the Jewish temple, which, after their long peregrinations, were respectively deposited in the Christian Church of Jerusalem" (chapter 41).

It is not likely, though possible, that the golden candlestick may still be hidden in some secret corner or recess of the church. More probably it has been stolen, or perhaps taken away by the Persians when the city was stormed by them, A.D. 614, or by some subsequent conqueror of the Holy City.

Which Was the Candlestick Exhibited in the Triumphal Arch?

While there is no doubt that the candlestick in the triumphal procession was got out of the temple, we have no information anywhere showing what particular one it was. The following are the sacred candlesticks used in the sanctuary:—

1. *The tabernacle candlestick,* which, after serving its day, was stored as a relic in Solomon's temple (1 Kings 8:4; 2 Chron. 5:5).

2. *The ten candlesticks made for Solomon's temple,* five of which stood on the right hand, and five on the left, of the holy place. These ten candlesticks were cut in pieces and carried by Nebuchadnezzar to Babylon (2 Kings 24:13–15).

The tabernacle candlestick and the tabernacle itself, and its other holy vessels are not mentioned as included in the temple treasures which Nebuchadnezzar took away, and must have escaped his notice, probably being stowed away in some out-of-the-way and unexplored chamber. But even if he had taken them, it does not follow on that account that they were lost to the Jews, for the treasures carried to Babylon were restored by Cyrus to the temple (Ezra 5:14, 15).

The ten candlesticks, though cut in pieces (2 Kings 24:13–15), were not so destroyed as to render them incapable of being restored to their original condition, for they were returned as above by Cyrus to the second temple, the one rebuilt by Zerubbabel.

The ten candlesticks again taken away from the temple.—In the year B.C. 170 Antiochus Epiphanes took away the golden vessels and other treasures of the temple (1 Maccabees 1:20, 21). As no mention is made of the tabernacle and its holy vessels, the probability is that they escaped the notice of Antiochus, as they had done that of Nebuchadnezzar.

3. *The candlestick presented to the temple by Judas Maccabeus.*—In the year B.C. 165 Judas Maccabeus expelled the Syrians and restored the

. . . One bud shall be under the first pair of branches extending from the lampstand, a second bud under the second pair, and a third bud under the third pair—six branches in all. The buds and branches shall all be of one piece with the lampstand, hammered out of pure gold.

Then make its seven lamps and set them up on it so that they light the space in front of it. Its wick trimmers and trays are to be of pure gold. A talent of pure gold is to be used for the lampstand and all these accessories. See that you make them according to the pattern shown you on the mountain (Exod. 25:31–40).

*After subduing Egypt,
Antiochus returned in the
one hundred forty-third
year. He went up against
Israel and came to
Jerusalem with a strong
force. He arrogantly
entered the sanctuary
and took the golden altar,
the lampstand for the
light, and all its utensils
(1 Macc. 1:20–21)*

sanctuary. He furnished the temple, we are told, with new holy vessels. "He made up the sanctuary, and the things that were within the temple, and hallowed the court. They made also new holy vessels, and unto the temple they brought the candlestick, the altar of burnt offerings, and of incense, and the Table" (1 Maccabees 4:48, 49). There was thus in the sanctuary as restored by Judas Maccabeus, as there had been in the tabernacle, only one candlestick, and not ten as there had been in Solomon's temple.

4. *The candlestick or candlesticks in Herod's temple.*—No mention is made of Herod having made golden vessels for the holy place of his temple; and it is generally taken for granted that he transferred those of the second temple to his own. We are strongly of opinion that he did not transfer the holy vessels of the second temple, supplied by Judas Maccabeus, for use in his own, but provided new golden vessels for the holy place of his temple, as he had provided everything else pertaining to the temple at his own expense. As there is no mention, as we have already noticed, of either Nebuchadnezzar or Epiphanes having removed the tabernacle candlestick from its resting-place in the temple, it is almost certain, as the priests were sure to know where it was stored, to have been removed by them for safe deposit in the Herodian temple. And as the candlestick and other golden vessels in use in the holy place of the second temple in the days of the Maccabees, were not, as we are convinced, transferred for use in that of Herod, they would also, as sacred relics, along with those of the tabernacle be deposited by the priests in the Herodian temple.

These two candlesticks, the one of the tabernacle and the one in use in the second temple (the one presented by Judas Maccabeus), at the time we are speaking of, are the only two holy place candlesticks known to have been in the second temple in the days of the Maccabees, and, of course, the only two that could have been removed to Herod's temple.

We can scarcely doubt that these two candlesticks were the two which came into the possession of

Titus. There are no other two we can possibly think of, or of which we can find any trace. The ten candlesticks which were used in Solomon's temple, and also for some time in the second temple, having, as we have seen (B.C. 170) been taken away by Antiochus.

During the assault on the upper city, "one of the priests," we are told, "delivered to Titus from the walls of the holy house two candlesticks, like to those that lay in the holy house, with tables and cisterns, and vials, all made of solid gold, and very heavy (Josephus *Wars*, 6.8, 3). Observe, they were not the candlesticks *in use* in the holy place of the temple, *but only like them*, and, of course, could have been no others than those of the tabernacle and the second temple (in the time of the Maccabees), taken from the deposit chambers in Herod's temple where, with other sacred relics, they had been placed.

One of these must have been the one that was carried in the triumphal procession. But which? The table which, along with the two candlesticks, the priest delivered to Titus, was, we are told by Josephus, of many talents weight, and of course was the one carried along with the candlestick in the triumphal procession.

Josephus occasionally is given to exaggerate, and we think there can be little doubt that he overstates the weight of the table. What number of talents may be considered many here? Certainly not fewer than from ten to twenty. If only ten, then the table would be worth about £50,000, or if twenty, then about £100,000, either sum much greater than we can reasonably suppose the table to have been worth.

As the candlestick shown on the Arch of Titus was rather larger than the table, it is taken for granted that the candlestick was likewise of many talents weight, and of course, like the table, would be worth from fifty to one hundred thousand pounds. If so, it could not have been the tabernacle candlestick,—so argue those who hold it must have been another. However, even though it could be shown that the table, as stated by Josephus, was of many talents weight, it does not follow that the candlestick must necessarily have been of about equal weight.

A talent of pure gold is to
be used for the lampstand
and all these accessories
(Exod. 25:39).

The only sure data we have to guide us as to the weight of the holy place candlesticks is that of the weight of the tabernacle candlestick, the prototype of the others. It weighed rather less than one talent (Exod. 25:39), and was worth about £5000. The ten of the holy place of Solomon's temple were undoubtedly made after the pattern of that of the tabernacle, and if so, each would be of the same weight, which would give a value of £50,000 for the ten. It is not in the least likely that the one gifted to the second temple by Judas Maccabeus, and which also would be made after the pattern of the divine original in the tabernacle, would be otherwise than about the same weight as it, and of those of Solomon's temple.

It is true that a talent of gold forms but a small block, but the candlestick, though made of pure gold and its parts of solid gold (we mean not merely gilded), must have been hollow, and this would account for about a talent of gold making a candle-stick of the size and shape of the tabernacle one, and also of the others which were made undoubtedly after the pattern of this their divine prototype.

In favor of the candlestick carried in the triumphal procession being of many talents' weight is the circumstance that eight men are represented as carrying it. But this is no decisive proof of its being of such weight, for if only of about one talent of weight according to our opinion, eight men might have been employed in carrying it. We cannot judge of the weight of trophies carried in a triumphal procession by the number of their bearers, since it is esteemed a great honor to act in this capacity. Arrangements are generally made to admit of as many men as can conveniently share the honor. To the same purpose is the circumstance that the weight of a triumphal car, and that of the number of men riding in it, cannot be judged by the number of horses or men drawing the carriage.

Of the two candlesticks delivered to Titus that of the tabernacle would undoubtedly appear the more ancient, and the prototype of the other, as it really was, and of the ten of Solomon's temple. So there can be little doubt the Titus would select it for exhibition in the triumphal procession.

From all the circumstances we have indicated we are convinced that it was the tabernacle candlestick that was carried in the triumphal procession, sculptured on the Arch of Titus, and sometime after deposited in the temple of Peace at Rome, where it remained in safety and honor for four centuries; was then transferred to Carthage where it remained for nearly one hundred years; thereafter removed to Constantinople; and finally found a resting-place in the Church of the Holy Sepulcher in Jerusalem. There, if not fallen a prey to some thief or invader, it is awaiting its resurrection by some fortunate and happy discoverer.

The tabernacle candlestick and Mount Nebo.— If it be historically true that the tabernacle candlestick was hid in a cave of Mount Nebo in the days of Jeremiah as some writers hold, then our contention regarding it falls to the ground. They tells us that Jeremiah, previous to his setting out for Egypt, took the tabernacle and its holy vessels to this famous mount, and there hid them in a cave. Their opinion is founded on the following passage in the second book of Maccabees: "It is also found in the records that the prophet commanded them that were carried away to take of the fire as it had been signified" (2:1). It was also contained in the sacred writing that the prophet, being warned of God, commanded that the tabernacle and the ark go with him, as he went forth into the mountain where Moses climbed up and saw the heritage of God. "And when Jeremy came thither, he found an hollow cave, wherein he laid the tabernacle, and the ark, and the altar of incense, and so stopped the door" (vv. 4, 5).

There can be little doubt that this passage is legendary. The learned Prideaux considers it fabulous. While it might be considered possible in the troubling times in Jerusalem, when the city and the land were harassed by Babylonian armies, to carry away a trifle or two, it can scarcely be conceived possible that the tabernacle and its holy vessels could be carried away to a cave in Mount Pisgah, seeing that no fewer than six wagons drawn by twelve oxen were required to transport the tabernacle from place to place in the wilderness. We hold the passage to be as we have said legendary. But even were it historically true, it will be observed that there is no mention in it of the golden candlestick, so that our contention with respect to it is not in the least affected by the passage.

INDEX TO SCRIPTURE REFERENCES

OLD TESTAMENT

Exodus

Page

13:20–22 .... 165, 166
13:21 165
13:22 166
14:1–13 166
14:19 164
14:24 170
15:1–21 166
16:33 76
16:34 76
20:24 .... 49, 82
25 25
25:1–7 4
25:8 4
25:9 1
25:10 183
25:10–22 75
25:11 .... 49, 76
25:15 75
25:17 76
25:18 77
25:18–22 77
25:19 77
25:20 .... 77, 78
25:22 77
25:23 58
25:24 58
25:25 .... 59, 182
25:27 59
25:28 59

25:29 .... 59, 60
25:31 .... 67, 68
25:31–38 68
25:32 68
25:33 68
25:34 .... 68, 69, 70
25:39 .... 67, 214
25:40 1
26:1 ... 28, 30, 34, 36, 37, 201
26:1–15 36
26:2 28
26:3 25
26:4 .... 25, 26
26:5 .... 25, 26
26:6 25
26:7 .... 28, 201
26:8 28
26:9 .... 29, 193
26:12 .... 31, 190, 201
26:13 .... 30, 201, 202
26:14 32
26:15 36
26:16 .... 6, 12
26:18 .... 4, 12
26:19 .... 4, 6
26:19–25 4
26:20 .... 4, 12
26:21 4
26:22–25 12
26:23 .... 17, 188
26:25 4
26:26 17

26:26–29 13
26:27 17
26:28 ..... 13, 194, 195, 197
26:30 .... 1, 4
26:31 .... 4, 35
26:31–37 34
26:32 4
26:33 .... 27, 197
26:34 188
27:1 48
27:1–8 49
27:2 49
27:3 .... 50, 51
27:4 49
27:5 49
27:8 1
27:9–19 41
27:10 41
27:17–19 42
27:18 147
27:20 71
27:21 71
27:27 9
28 87
28:1 85
28:1–43 .... 84, 88, 94
28:2–43 106
28:6–12 99
28:10 .... 99, 102
28:12 99
28:15–30 102
28:16 182

28:17 102
28:30 104
28:32 95
28:33–35 95
28:34 95
28:35 96
28:36 109
28:37 109
28:38 110
28:39 ....90, 91, 92
28:40 ....91, 93
28:42 89
29:38 120
29:38–46 129
30:3 62
30:4 62
30:6 62
30:7 71
30:7–11 130
30:8 71
30:10 ....64, 137
30:13 9
30:15 9
30:16 10
30:19 55
30:20 56
30:21 56
30:34 63
31:1–6 1
33:9 169
33:15 170
35:11 201
35:18 31
35:25 ....25, 28
35:35 25
36 4
36:1 ....18, 24, 25
36:1–15 24
36:6 ....19, 24
36:7 ....19, 24
36:8 28
36:13 201
36:14 24

36:15 24
36:33 ....13, 15, 195
37 4
37:17 68
37:20 70
38 4
38:1–7 49
38:8 ....54, 55
38:10 41
38:24 19
38:25 9
38:27 ....4, 6, 8, 10 17
38:28 43
38:29 41
38:29–31 41
39:1–31 106
39:2 99
39:4 99
39:5 100
39:8–21 102
39:9 182
39:13 102
39:15–21 104
39:22 95
39:27 91
39:27–29 89
39:28 ....91, 93, 108
39:29 ....91, 92
39:31 109
40:22 58
40:23 ....58, 59
40:24 67

LEVITICUS
1 ....118, 120
1:1 79
1:11 119
2 121
2:11 121
2:13 121
3 122
4 ....120, 123, 125
4:3–13 123
4:3–28 123
4:12 50

4:13–22 124
4:20 125
4:22–27 124
4:26 125
4:27–35 124
4:31 125
4:35 125
5 ....120, 123, 125
5:1–19 125
6 ....120, 123, 125
6:10 129
6:11 129
6:13 51
7:30 122
7:31–34 122
7:32 122
8:9–12 110
8:14–16 120
8:15 51
9:8–12 120
9:18 122
9:24 51
10:2 170
12:6 120
13:46–59 126
14 126
14:19 120
15 126
16 135
16:1–34 120
16:4 ....95, 136
16:11 85
16:11–25 120
16:18 ....64, 137
16:23 202
16:24 140
16:29 135
16:31 135
21 84
21:23 84
22:17–26 118
24:2 71
24:5–9 59

24:7 60
24:8 60
26:9 59

NUMBERS
1:46 9
1:47–50 9
1:53 37
2:2 ....151, 155
2:2–10 152
2:10–17 152
2:18–28 152
2:25–29 152
3:11–16 9
3:12 113
3:23 152
3:25–36 201
3:29 151
3:31 75
3:35 152
3:38 151
3:39 113
3:40 9
3:41 9
3:43 113
3:46–51 113
4 114
4:5 80
4:6 80
4:7 59
4:15 ....75, 80, 156
4:47 113
4:48 113
7:89 79
8:4 70
8:5–23 114
10 156
10:14–16 156
10:17 ....156, 157
10:18 157
10:20 157
10:21 157
10:22 157
10:24 157

10:25–27 157
10:33 ....75, 80, 156
10:33–36 80
12:15 126
15:28 125
15:37–40 97
17:10 76
18:21 115
23:8–10 156
24:5 156
24:6 156
24:8 156
24:9 156
28 121
28:9 120
28:10 120
28:11–16 120
28:16–26 120
29:7 135
29:8 135

DEUTERONOMY
1:30 167
1:31 167
3:2 182
3:11 181
17:8–12 115
18:1 115
18:2 115
31:9 75
31:25 75
31:26 76
32:10 115
33:10 ....86, 114

JOSHUA
3:3 75
3:4 151
5:10 80
8:31 122
18:1 80
21 115
21:41 86

JUDGES
20:26–28 79

1 SAMUEL
3:12–14 91
4:11 80
4:11–18 91
5:3–5 80
6:19–21 80
17:4 182

2 SAMUEL
6:12–16 80
6:17 122

1 KINGS
1:50–53 52
6:35 34
6:37 35
7:26 182
8:4 211
8:6 75
8:8 75
8:9 76
8:12 206
8:62 122

2 KINGS
24:13–15 211

1 CHRONICLES
23 115

2 CHRONICLES
3:3 ....181, 182
4:5 182
5:5 ....80, 211
17:7–9 114
29:34 ....86, 114

EZRA
5:14 211
5:15 211

NEHEMIAH
6:3 21
9:19 167
10:37 115

JOB
13:15 173

PSALMS
5:7 45
18:2 175
22:6 33
23:4 173
24:3 95
24:4 95
27:4–6 45
36:8 45
40:6 120
50:23 96
77:53 166
78:52 166
80:1 ....78, 165
91:2 175
100:4 ....45, 49
105:39 ....167, 194
107:7 166
116 45
118:27 49
119:105 172
121:6 ....167, 194
132 45
141:2 64

PROVERBS
6:22 172
6:23 172
15:8 131

ISAIAH
1:10–17 131
4:5 171
9:6 100
11:5 92
22:22 100
32:2 174
35:10 177

49:16 100
53:2 33
60:1 171

EZEKIEL
16:9–15 33
40:5 184
42:13 202
42:14 202
40:5 181
41:8 181
43:13 182

DANIEL
4:35 173

ZECHARIAH
14:20 110

NEW TESTAMENT
MATTHEW
28:20 82

LUKE
1:9–11 63
1:10 131
24:50–52 35

JOHN
1:14 39
1:18 175
3:3–5 56
15:3 56
16:13 172
17:17 56
19:23 91

ACTS
1:9–11 35
7:44 4

ROMANS
3:25 ....76, 77
12:1 119

1 CORINTHIANS
3:16 38
6:11 57
6:19 10
6:20 10

2 CORINTHIANS
12:9 174

GALATIANS
3:13 10

EPHESIANS
2:19–22 23
2:20–22 39
2:22 37
5:26 56

COLOSSIANS
1:20 52
1:21 52

TITUS
3:5 57

HEBREWS
1:1 175
1:2 175
5:1 120
8:5 ....1, 4
9:2 34
9:3 35
9:4 76
9:12–16 125
9:36 34
10:4 125
10:6 120
10:22 56
13:12 127

1 PETER
1:12 78
1:18 10

1 JOHN
2:2 127

REVELATION
1:4 72
3:12 22
5:8 64
7:9 93
19:8 ....89, 93
21:16 ....73, 148
21:23 ....72, 174